Advance Praise for *Click 2 Save: The Digital Ministry Bible*

Just as 500 years ago the Gutenberg printing press made the dissemination of information inexpensive and easy, galvanizing the public opinion that fueled the Reformation, so the internet and the explosion of digital media have connected people as never before. Elizabeth Drescher and Keith Anderson have created a kind of digital-media-for-dummies guide. They have invited us to see digital social media as an opportunity for ministry and the proclamation of the gospel. They explain the basics for novices, and offer strategies for veterans. For any who want to proclaim a message of hope to those young and old, churched and unchurched, near and far in this digital age, these tools are going to be indispensable.

—Bishop Michael Rinehart
Texas-Louisiana Gulf Coast Synod
Evangelical Lutheran Church in America

Drescher and Anderson have pulled social media in the church back from the cliffs of marketing and positioned it as a tool for doing ministry well. In the language of faith, they have found the "incarnational" in the rush of electrons that deliver the ever growing number of virtual messages. Social media will never "save" the church, but as Drescher and Anderson show, it might just teach us a thing or two about building relationships as Jesus would.

—Martin Davis
Director, The Congregational Resource Guide
The Alban Institute

In *Click 2 Save: The Digital Ministry Bible*, Drescher and Anderson guide readers in creating and implementing a digital ministry strategy that will help build and sustain community online and face-to-face. The idea of using social media can still seem a bit strange and daunting to novices, but reading this book is like having two kind friends stop by for a chat. As the authors share their own and others' stories about the use of Facebook, Twitter, and LinkedIn, they invite even the most tenta[ ] vibrant, global conversation on faith and sp[ ]

Autho[ ]
Assistant Professor of Orgar[ ]
Gannon University, Erie, Pennsylvania

D1280385

Read this book immediately to discover a humanizing approach to unleash the "social" in digital social media.

—Robert V. Taylor
Author of *A New Way to Be Human:*
7 Spiritual Pathways to Becoming Fully Alive

As an aging baby-boomer ministering in the midst of a major university, I often find myself literally at sea in the waves of social media. Keith Anderson and Elizabeth Drescher have done an exceptional job of delineating the digital landscape, explaining why it is important to understand and master, and providing useful tools to accomplish that essential task. It is simply a gift to ministers of all generations who wish to understand, enter, and explore this brave new world.

—The Rev. Dr. Wendel "Tad" Meyer
The Memorial Church
Harvard University, Cambridge, Massachusetts

This is *the* must-read book on social media ministry. All church leaders will benefit from its clarity, organization, and practicality. Readers will appreciate the theological and pastoral sensitivities the authors bring as they frame social media inextricably within the revitalization of the church's mission.

—Lovett H. Weems, Jr.
Director, Lewis Center for Church Leadership
Wesley Theological Seminary, Washington, DC

Skillfully interweaving real stories and sage advice with hands-on tools, these gifted writers have produced a work that will greatly benefit clergy and congregations moving into the new digital world. I am grateful that they share their wisdom and experience with the rest of us—both digital natives and those dipping their toes into social media for the first time. That they nuance their recommendations with pastoral vision and theological insight is a significant bonus.

—Verity A. Jones
Director, New Media Project
Union Theological Seminary in the City of New York

Click 2 Save cuts through the marketing jargon and technical detail to give you what you really need to make sense of this rapidly changing world of digital ministry. This invaluable resource is both a "why-to" and a "how-to" for all who minister in the twenty-first century. The Message remains the message, but Drescher and Anderson help us understand how that message is measured online in likes, views, follows and transformed communities.

—Bob Carlton
Blogger and consultant on digital publishing and ministry

Click 2 Save is a lifesaver for those in ministry who know they need to learn about social media but all too often only find advertising experts who know nothing of the needs of clergy. At last there is a resource written for Christian leaders looking to use social media, written with references to theologians and pastors who are using social media in their daily lives. *Click 2 Save* is relevant to those who know nothing about social media, and those like me who use social media but are grateful for a resource both mindful and spiritual.

—Bob Craigue
Director, The Media Center
Andover-Newton Theological School, Newton Centre, Massachusetts

CLICK 2 SAVE

The Digital Ministry Bible

CLICK 2 SAVE

The Digital Ministry Bible

BY ELIZABETH DRESCHER
AND KEITH ANDERSON

Morehouse Publishing
NEW YORK · HARRISBURG · DENVER

Unless otherwise noted, the Scripture quotations contained herein are from the New Revised Standard Version Bible, copyright © 1989 by the Division of Christian Education of the National Council of Churches of Christ in the U.S.A. Used by permission. All rights reserved.

Morehouse Publishing, 4775 Linglestown Road, Harrisburg, PA 17112

Morehouse Publishing, 445 Fifth Avenue, New York, NY 10016

Morehouse Publishing is an imprint of Church Publishing Incorporated.
www.churchpublishing.org

Cover design by Laurie Klein Westhafer
Illustrations by Angelo Lopez © 2012. Used by permission.
Typeset by Rose Design

Library of Congress Cataloging-in-Publication Data

Drescher, Elizabeth.
 Click 2 save : the digital ministry bible / by Elizabeth Drescher and Keith Anderson.
    p. cm.
 Includes bibliographical references.
  ISBN 978-0-8192-2774-4 (pbk. : alk. paper)—ISBN 978-0-8192-2775-1 (ebook) 1. Internet in church work. 2. Social media. 3. Church work. I. Anderson, Keith. II. Title. III. Title: Click two save. IV. Title: Click to save.
 BR99.74.D73 2012
 253.0285'675--dc23
                        2012001459

Printed in the United States of America

10 9 8 7 6 5 4 3 2 1

For Our Networked Families and Faith Communities

CONTENTS

ACKNOWLEDGMENTS

Every writing project, however many hours a writer might spend holed up before a glowing computer screen, is the work of many, the kindnesses of encouraging friends and rich insights of content sources all feeding the finished work. This networked participation insists that writing is always a collaborative process. This project has been particularly so, not just because it is the work of two authors, but because our work was possible only because so many friends, colleagues, and very perfect strangers shared their experiences with social media in the context of ministry with us and contributed much to our thinking about what digital ministry is and what it looks like when done well. You will meet many of these people in the pages that follow, and we are deeply indebted to each of them for their contributions to this project. We would also like to acknowledge a number of people who influenced our work on "deep background," as it were: Greg Troxell, Meredith Gould, Mary Hess, Patricia Carr, The Rev. Gene Anderson, The Rev. Penny Nash, Unvirtuous Abbey, The Rev. Martin Malzahn, Katie Osweiler, and Linda Sevier.

We are grateful to our keen-eyed, challenging, and affirming editor, Stephanie Spellers. She brought a quality of editorial guidance that comes as much from her experience with the sort of relational, networked, incarnational leadership we explore in the book as from her remarkable skills with words, ideas, and their organization in print. Likewise, we have appreciated the support of the team at Church Publishing, especially William Falvey, Jeff Hamilton, Ryan Masteller, Lillian Schell Ort, and Lorraine Simonello, whose many efforts put this book in your hand. And, we are beyond excited that CPI invited Angelo Lopez to contribute the wonderful illustrations throughout the book.

Many of the concepts in the pages ahead were first developed for and tested in conversations with people from the Episcopal Dioceses of Missouri and Northwestern Pennsylvania, the Roman Catholic Diocese of San Jose, the New England and Rocky Mountain Synods of the Evangelical Lutheran

Church in America, Andover-Newton Theological School, The Lutheran Theological Seminary at Philadelphia, United Theological Seminary, St. Vincent College, and a number of churches and other organizations in and around Boston and the San Francisco Bay Area. We are both grateful for these opportunities to share early versions of our work with thoughtful, engaged digital-ministers-in-formation throughout the wider church.

Elizabeth is deeply indebted to Kelly Simons, who does so much to make the time and space for research and writing on projects like this one possible. She would also like to thank Deborah Lohse, Paul Crowley, William Dohar, Gary Macy, and students in the Graduate Program in Pastoral Ministries at Santa Clara University for their continuing support. Special thanks, as well, are owed to Jim Naughton and Rebecca Wilson of Canticle Communications, Lisa Webster and Evan Derkacz at *Religion Dispatches*, Donna Freitas, and The Rt. Rev. Mary Gray-Reeves, bishop of the Episcopal Diocese of El Camino Réal.

Keith wishes to thank Jennifer Anderson for her amazing love and support, and to dedicate his work on this project to their children, Ellie, Finn, Dulcie and Tess. He would also like to thank his mother, Rose Hamelin, and father, Rick Anderson, for being advocates for education and supporting him in his call to ministry. Keith extends his grateful appreciation to the people of the Lutheran Church of the Redeemer in Woburn, Massachusetts, whose vision for sharing the Gospel inspired many of the ideas and practices in these pages and whose support and encouragement has been essential in the writing of this book. Heartfelt thanks are also due to Elly and Kathy Alboim, Susan Pursch, The Rev. Scott Howard, The Rev. Mark Huber, and The Rev. Arthur Scherer.

INTRODUCTION
Digital Pilgrimage

What's this chapter about? How a Lutheran pastor and an Episcopal professor connected through social media and what that has to do with this book, with a bit on the chapters ahead.

OUR DIGITAL SOCIAL MEDIA CONNECTION developed a few years ago, just after Elizabeth published an article in the online magazine *Religion Dispatches*. The article was about the encouragement of Pope Benedict XVI for Roman Catholic priests to enter the rapidly developing digital religious landscape by blogging on faith and spirituality whenever they could. While the article lauded the pope for his concern that the church be actively represented among the many voices in the religious blogosphere, it also pointed out that the pontiff had missed the social media mark to a considerable degree because he had assumed that digital social media functioned in the same top-down, one-to-many way as mass broadcast media. The inexperience with digital practice illustrated in the pope's letter was hardly unique to the Roman Catholic Church. Mainline churches of all stripes were more or less bumbling into the digital domain, despite what turned out to be native gifts for relational communication that are ideally suited to life in the Digital Age. Elizabeth

WHAT IS DIGITAL MINISTRY?

Digital ministry is the set of practices that extend spiritual care, formation, prayer, evangelism, and other manifestations of grace into online spaces like Facebook, Twitter, and YouTube, where more and more people gather to nurture, explore, and share their faith today.

It can also refer to these practices in both online and offline spaces as they are influenced by the networked, relational character of digital culture in general.

eventually explored mainline engagement with new media in much greater depth in *Tweet If You* ♥ *Jesus: Practicing Church in the Digital Reformation.*

But the article on the pope's entree into the digital domain did more than anchor the subsequent book. It also brought us together as colleagues in what we now think of as "digital ministry"—colleagues whom it is all but impossible to imagine might have connected before the age of digital social media. In the weeks after the *Religion Dispatches* piece came out, Keith emailed Elizabeth to share some insights from his work on the role of social media in his own church in the form of a presentation he'd recently given to a group of Lutheran clergy that included a couple quotes from her article.

Keith's presentation, "From Gutenberg to Zuckerberg: How Social Media is Changing the Church," moved beyond the commonly offered religious repackaging of marketing advice for profit-making businesses to locate social media participation in the theologies and spiritual practices that shaped and continue to animate the Lutheran Church. And, not for nothing, it had a way cool picture of Charlton Heston holding an iPhone version of the Ten Commandments that Elizabeth was able to poach for an upcoming talk on the Bible and social media.

So it was that, from three thousand miles and a denomination away, a Lutheran pastor and blogger became a colleague and friend to an Episcopal writer and educator. Now, a couple years later, we have become collaborators on *Click 2 Save: The Digital Ministry Bible*, sharing the fruit of an extended conversation about the role of new media not only in our own denominations, but across the church as it attempts to remain engaged in a rapidly changing world. Together, we have become digital pilgrims of a sort, traveling, sometimes together, sometimes apart, through the byways of the rapidly changing digital landscape and sharing tales of who we meet and what we find along the way.

We begin with this story not only because it seems a particularly charming, Digital Age way for two writers to come together on a project, but also because it says so much about how relationships are formed, how knowledge is created and shared, and, ultimately, how faith is reinforced and extended in the world today. Over the course of the past two years, we have shared resources and connected one another to colleagues. When Elizabeth put together a relatively impromptu tweeted, global Pentecost prayer service in 2010, Keith and a few members of his congregation, the Lutheran Church of the Redeemer in Woburn, Massachusetts, joined in. So, it's fair to say that we've worshipped together as well.

All of this unlikely interaction has taken place between a pastor and a religious studies scholar whose face-to-face interaction was, until pretty far along in the writing of this book, limited to flickering images on weekly Google+ video "hangouts." Which is to say that without digital social media, this book would absolutely not have been written. More significantly, the church would be a teeny bit smaller, a teeny bit less connected, a teeny bit less catholic. Multiply that by the healthy percentage of mainline Protestants and Catholics among the more than eight hundred million Facebook users, and you get a sense of the impact of social media on the church and on Christian ministry today. It is the reality of our own digitally enabled relationship that is at the root of *Click 2 Save* and of our enthusiasm for the potential that new social media have for enriching and extending the mission of the church. In the chapters ahead, we lay out what we see as a strategic approach to living out that potential.

CHAPTER 1: REMAPPING OUR WORLDS

While we wouldn't go as far as to say that effective engagement will *save* a rapidly declining church on its own, we are confident that much of the hope for revitalizing our churches and sustaining their good work in the world is related to the ability of leaders in ministry to engage people exactly where they are. And "where they are" increasingly includes social media spaces like Facebook, Twitter, YouTube, and LinkedIn.

This means that everything's a bit topsy-turvy these days, with all the world's major newspapers offering religious insight and education; bloggers of all stripes sermonating and otherwise opining on theology, spirituality, and religious life; websites and smartphone apps offering opportunities to pray, meditate, sing, confess, learn about religions, and mount arguments for and against them. Religious formation and spiritual enrichment are now all over the digital map. Chapter 1 begins, then, by exploring how digital media have remapped the world we all share, constructing not only new worldviews that challenge long-held notions of geography and place, but also reorganizing relational possibilities across the planet.

Once we've spent some time mapping the evolving digital planet, we move in Chapter 1 to describe the inhabitants of its most robust communities, Facebook and Twitter, by way of highlighting the differences between so-called "digital natives" and the people we typically see at church on Sunday. It's a huge world with lots and lots of people, so the view is from somewhere above ten thousand feet, but our hope is to orient you to the general terrain so you'll be better prepared to gather resources, make connections, and enter conversations that will help you to develop a social media strategy for your church or religious organization.

Travel across this new landscape of social networking sites is on the rise across generations, demographic groups, and around the globe. Recent research by the Pew Internet & American Life Project and Neilson has illustrated this growth in the population in general, but it also points to particular practices of digital engagement that are significant for mainline churches and ministers who wish to connect with believers and seekers alike. Chapter 1 helps to differentiate the "natives" and "immigrants" who inhabit online communities and networks, as this matters in the context of ministry.[1]

> Whether or not we choose to bring our ministries actively into the world shaped by social media, citizens of that world always have the opportunity to bring us into it by sharing commentary, images, and other content about us and our churches or organizations.

What Chapter 1 should make clear, then, is that, as it has been reshaped by new social media, the world is a very different place than it was even five or ten years ago. Certainly, it's very, very different from the 1950s and '60s worlds with which many mainline churchgoers still identify and which, therefore, continue to have a strong influence on church practice. Back then, in the last great growth period for mainline Christianity in America and globally, people got their religion from the local church and their news from Walter Cronkite, and the two zones for the most part maintained a polite, respectful disengagement. Sure, the local paper probably had a religion section, but that mostly covered service times and socials at neighborhood churches, setting aside any potentially divisive theological debate. The idea was to reinforce religious participation as a civic virtue, not to sow religious disagreement. The proliferation of traditional news media outlets as well the ability for anyone to self-publish through blogs, YouTube, and other social media sites, has led to an increasingly rich, sometimes overwhelming, sometimes contentious, but certainly changed religious world.

The map of the world before social media—the world defined by the practices of the Industrial and Broadcast Ages—showed a world defined by distinction, separation, clear boundaries between this land and that, this community and the others, *our* church and *theirs*. As we'll see, the new world shaped by social networking is mapped relationally. It's defined by the flow of ideas across all kinds of boundaries. Navigating in this new world calls on a nuanced understanding of the terrain and the customs of the locals. We'll begin to mark the major byways, landmarks, and populations across the socially networked globe in Chapter 1.

CHAPTER 2: THE REAL PRESENCE

Once you've got a handle on the differences among people using social media and the range of social media locales in which they interact—especially as these differ from your face-to-face ministry context—developing a clearer sense of how you and your church want to be present in social media contexts is critical. Chapter 2 focuses on how to communicate an authentic representation of self and ministry that humanizes both individuals and communities. After all, before anyone walks through the door of your church or community service site or pub ministry, odds are that they've already taken a look at your website and moseyed over to your Facebook page. They know something of you and your community, and you want that "something" to be real and meaningful—far beyond the "just the facts, ma'am" tone of all too many church websites and Facebook pages.

The good news is that achieving "real presence" in social media spaces is far less theologically fraught for mainline churches than sorting out the mysteries of the Eucharist has been over the centuries. Drawing on Keith's pastoral experience and that of colleagues in ministry, Chapter 2 will guide you through the basics of establishing an authentic voice and taking up practices of relational communication that ground an effective strategy for social media ministry.

> We are ministers, not marketers, so our presence in digital spaces must be very clearly defined in terms of authentic ministry—authentic connection with others from whom we have nothing personally or institutionally to gain and to whom we have much to offer.

CHAPTER 3: I LOVE TO TELL THE STORY

Once you have a sense of how best to be authentically present in social media spaces generally, it's important to nuance that presence for a specific social media locale. The idea here is to focus on the features of a particular platform that can best help you to tell your story and that of your faith community. In *Click 2 Save*, we highlight what we see as the major social media platforms based on numbers of active participants, our best guess at durability in the rapidly changing digital landscape, and compatibility with traditional and emerging mainline ministry practice. The platforms we discuss in Chapter 3 include:

- Facebook—*www.facebook.com*
- Twitter—*www.twitter.com*
- LinkedIn—*www.linkedin.com*
- Blogs—e.g., *www.wordpress.com*; *www.blogger.com*; *www.posterous. com*; *www.tumblr.com*
- YouTube—*www.youtube.com*
- Foursquare—*www.foursquare.com*

This chapter will help you to decide which combination of social media platforms will be most effective for you by providing a range of criteria for decision making, such as congregational style and strengths, intended conversation partners (i.e., age groups, location, members, potential members), congregational goals, level of skill, and available time.

One way to think about your approach to various platforms is to consider how you present yourself, your ministry, and your faith community in different local settings. If you're a spiritual director, for instance, you're unlikely to dole out morsels of spiritual wisdom online at the local coffee house. But you probably are inclined to express a general attentiveness to those you encounter—perhaps a certain warmth toward the latte-slinger behind the counter—that reflects something true about your spiritual values. This is much the sort of presence you'll want to cultivate on platforms like Twitter, while in spaces that allow for more extended exchange, like Facebook or, more still, blogs, you'll tell the story of your faith, your ministry, and your community somewhat differently. Chapter 3 will acquaint you with each of the major platforms, highlighting those features that will best open your story to others and introducing tools and tips to help as you continue to develop your social media strategy.

Please note: Our approach to these platforms is through the lens of digital ministry practice. So, our exploration of social media platforms in

Chapter 3 is meant to serve as a guide to ministry, not a manual on the technical features of each platform *per se*. While our discussions of various platforms will refer to key features and characteristics, and we will provide some basic definitions, we assume that readers have visited the social networking sites we discuss, and that they have a basic familiarity with how they work. If you have not done so already, it will be helpful as we move ahead together if you have set up basic Facebook and Twitter profiles. You can add accounts for other platforms as they make sense within your digital ministry strategy.

CHAPTER 4: PRACTICING THE ARTS OF DIGITAL MINISTRY

Given a good idea of who's where and what's what in the digital domain, a clearly articulated sense of presence, and an understanding of how and when to use various social media platforms, the art of networked, relational ministry in social media communities begins. We approach the art of digital ministry through a mode of digital participation that Elizabeth introduced in *Tweet If You ♥ Jesus*. There, she described life in the Digital Reformation—a revitalization of the church driven largely by the *ad hoc* spiritualities of ordinary believers influenced by digital social networking—as organized around four core practices she calls a "LACE":

- *Listening*—taking time to get to know people in social networks based on what they share in profiles, posts, tweets, and so on, rather than emphasizing the communication of your own message
- *Attending*—noticing and being present to the experiences and interests of others as they share themselves in digital spaces
- *Connecting*—reaching out to others in diverse communities in order to deepen and extend the networks that influence your digital spiritual practice
- *Engaging*—building relationships by sharing content, collaborating, and connecting people to others

This networked, relational LACE, Elizabeth argued, is a re-emerging mode of engagement that connects life in the ancient and medieval church to life in the church today, offering opportunities to enrich our relationships, our communities, and our churches after long centuries of increasing separation and distancing brought about by mass media and, in particular, broadcast media like radio, television, and movies.[2]

As we move in *Click 2 Save* to draw out the implications of the Digital Reformation for hands-on ministry practice, we explore the LACE more specifically through what we see as basic "arts of digital ministry":

- *Offering spiritual care* to others through practices of prayer, comfort, encouragement, and inspiration
- *Offering hospitality* by extending welcome, creating sacred space, respectfully evangelizing, and incorporating others into the church
- *Forming disciples* and enriching their spiritual lives through preaching, education, and small group ministries
- *Building community* by engaging others and helping to connect them to one another
- *Sharing public witness* through activism, social justice practices, advocacy in partnership with the marginalized and forgotten, and supporting the vitality of local communities

Chapter 4 also shares three detailed social media case studies. Two are from individual ministry leaders—the Reverend Nadia Bolz-Weber of the Lutheran mission church House for All Sinners and Saints in Denver, and the Reverend Matthew Moretz of St. Bartholomew's Episcopal Church in New York. Another is from an organization—the Massachusetts Council of Churches. Your strategy, whether for your personal ministry or for your church or other religious organization, will not of course be exactly like any of those we share. We offer them, however, as an illustration of the kinds of reflection that go into developing a social media strategy and the results this reflection can provide.

> "Approach social media as you would anything else in the church. If you have someone in your congregation who has gifts for it, try to make use of those gifts."
>
> —Emily Scott, Pastoral Minister
> St. Lydia's Church, New York

CONCLUSION: DIGITAL INCARNATION

When we started this project, we talked a lot about what the word "save" in the title meant to us. It's a tricky word for mainline Christians, who have had—at least since the end of overt colonialism—less evangelically oriented, less proselytizing traditions. We tend, that is, not to announce our faith too loudly lest doing so impinge on the beliefs of others. We don't generally call out the personal sinfulness of others and offer absolution within our churches. We don't make a point to articulate, often even privately, the distinctiveness of our denominational traditions.

Elizabeth tells the story of her grandmother, who, as the family passed the churches of other denominations in her small town on the way to "the true church," would sigh and say, "I don't know why those people even bother to get up early on a Sunday. They're all going to damnation anyway. May as well sleep in." (She said that in the car, of course, not on the sidewalk.) The fact that mainline Christians seldom even think such things anymore, focusing more on our commonality as Christians than theological differences across denominations, is surely all to the good.

But it also seems to be the case that our understandable embarrassment over the demeaning and divisive dismissal of other faiths that was tolerable in earlier times has turned into a stultifying silence about who we really are as mainline Christians and how our faith allows us to live with others in the world in remarkable, loving, and healing ways. This has only been exacerbated by what many see as a co-optation of the word "Christian" itself by more fundamentalist believers, whose often condemning approach to sharing the faith has sowed disdain and outright hostility toward all Christians. As a result, many people who believe in God and in fact participate in Christian communities prefer to identify as agnostic, as "spiritual but not religious," or as having "no religious belief in particular."[3]

Our perspective is that new social networking platforms enable us to extend the love of God to others in ways that make our mainline Christian traditions more authentically present in the world. This may not "save" other believers and seekers in the sense of converting them to our particular denominations, and it may not "save" our churches in terms of numerical and associated financial stability. But, as you'll see in the Conclusion, we think our participation in the new media landscape has a profoundly salvific effect nonetheless, saving God's church from a marginalization and irrelevance that prevents us from doing the work of love, compassion, and justice to which we are all called.

We began this chapter by noting that this book itself began in digital conversation. It might almost go without saying that this conversational mode continued as Keith and Elizabeth worked on the book, the ideas in each chapter being shaped through email, Facebook posts, tweets, documents swapped on Dropbox, and Google+ video chats. However, in order to manage the work and avoid creating a schizophrenic tone, we divided the chapters between us, and shared comments after each draft. This process has allowed us to produce a book that is very much a collaborative product, drawing upon something of a single authorial direction in each chapter, but nonetheless expressing a shared vision and voice.

Still, because we each also bring unique perspectives to our shared project, from time to time you'll see call-out boxes with short comments from one of us. Likewise, you'll find notes on terminology that might be new, and tips on practices and resources that can make your digital ministry easier. And, you'll find profiles of digital ministers we interviewed during the course of writing this book. What can we say? Keith is a digital native, and Elizabeth is pretty fully naturalized. Like more and more of the people you encounter in church and other ministries, we roll through the Digital Reformation with a lot of other voices and information in tow. We hope it'll make for lively reading that supports your developing digital ministry while modeling the modes of communication current in the digital domain.

ENOUGH ABOUT US:
ABOUT YOU, GENERALLY IN PARTICULAR

Writers typically write for a more or less imagined, composite reader—a "you" made up of a variety of backgrounds, characteristics, and experiences drawn from very different people. This is certainly true for *Click 2 Save*, which we address to the broad category of "leaders in ministry" that includes clergy and laypeople in both formal and informal ministry roles. We take a kind of "priesthood of all believers" understanding of readers of this book, assuming that each of us in the church is called to witness to and welcome others into the faith regardless of our title or role. In that sense, we're all leaders in ministry, our everyday lives enacting the relationship with God in Jesus Christ that is at the center of our faith. So, in the end, we see *Click 2 Save* as a book for disciples in general.

Click 2 Save also speaks to the very particular experiences, stories, and questions we both have encountered in our respective pastoral and educational ministries. It is drawn from conversations not just with the people we interviewed for the book, many of whom will be profiled in the pages ahead, but from ongoing conversations with colleagues, church members, and a rich blend of friends whom we regularly encounter in face-to-face and social media settings. Their questions about social media participation as it might help to address the challenges facing their various communities are very particular, very much located in the realities of sustaining small or large church communities; growing or declining service, community, and social justice programs; and tending established and emerging spiritual friendship networks.

One of the things we've learned as we've studied social media practice in religious contexts, talked with a wide range of practitioners, and mucked around in Facebook, Twitter, YouTube, LinkedIn, and so on ourselves is that there is no one-size-fits-all approach that will address the particular needs of each community or individual. But, of course, the beauty of new media is that it is endlessly adaptable, and this is exactly what we invite you to do with this book. In effect, we invite you to write *Click 2 Save* with us, using the information we share in light of your particular needs to develop a social media strategy for your specific ministry. At the end of each chapter you'll find space for this customizing of the ideas and approaches we share. We hope, too, that you'll visit the *Click 2 Save* Facebook page or Twitter feed to share your experience as you adapt and apply the ideas in the chapters ahead in your particular context.

As you get ready to develop a social media strategy for your church or religious organization, we will invite you to step back a bit and consider what motivates your social media participation and what you hope to accomplish by deepening your practice. The puzzle piece icon that appears throughout the book marks the spot for strategic reflection on the material covered in each chapter. If you're working with a group on social media strategy for your community—a practice we certainly encourage—you may want to copy the strategy page for participants.

You'll see other icons throughout the book that mark our comments on each other's ideas, profiles of digital ministers across the denominational spectrum in a variety of settings, social media tools that may be helpful in your digital ministry, definitions of social media terminology we use in the book, and quick tips for social media practice. Here are the icons you'll see in the pages ahead:

 Chapter summaries

 The basics on a social media platform including terminology and common practices

 Comments by Elizabeth

 Strategic reflection on your ministry context

 Comments by Keith

 Quick tips on social media practice

 Profiles of digital ministers

PIRATE THIS BOOK

Back in the day, political activist Abbie Hoffman wrote an ironic bestseller called *Steal This Book*, which aimed to promote the overthrow of the government by encouraging a number of ethically questionable and wholly illegal activities. That's hardly our agenda in *Click 2 Save*, but we do want you to make this book your own, to use it as a launch for conversations with friends, colleagues, parishioners, and others involved in the revitalization of mainline churches as they serve God in the world. We've come to almost all of the ideas we share in the book by way of such conversations, and we're very much looking forward to hearing your voice and seeing your community as we continue to develop our own digital ministries.

To get started, please take some time on your own or with friends and colleagues to reflect on the strategic questions below.

DIGITAL MINISTRY STRATEGY

Why do you think digital ministry is important for you and your church or other religious organization?

_____

_____

_____

_____

What are your personal and/or organizational goals for digital ministry?

_____

_____

_____

_____

How much time do you have for digital ministry?

_____

_____

_____

_____

Who will support you and/or join you in digital ministry?

_____

_____

_____

_____

What other resources are available for your digital ministry?

_____

_____

_____

_____

1

REMAPPING OUR WORLDS
How Social Media Have Transformed the Landscape

 Social media have remapped the world, pushing beyond all sorts of boundaries—geographic, demographic, and conceptual alike. In this chapter, we look at the new global, social world and the people who inhabit it as background to the upcoming discussion of participation in specific social media platforms from a faith and ministry perspective.

REMAPPING THE WORLD

Even if you happened to be off on a remote, Wi-Fi-disabled island vacation in the summer of 2011, by the time you sailed back to reality you surely caught the news that Facebook had grown to more than seven-hundred-fifty million users, eclipsing all other social networking communities. The surge in Facebook membership (which topped eight-hundred million as we were sending this manuscript to press) and the way it has begun to change our view of the world brings to mind the shift in mapmaking in the sixteenth century, after wider global travel and mechanistic mapmaking altered the reigning perception of the world. In the ancient and medieval worlds, a map was less a representation of geopolitical reality than it was an expression of the cultural terrain from the perspective of the mapmaker and his patrons. For example, the famous Hereford *Mappa Mundi* (or "map of the world") situates Jerusalem in the center, the Garden of Eden at the top (which is east on the map), and a variety of other biblical locales—Noah's ark, the Red Sea, Babylon—along with England, Scotland, and Ireland all out of geographical proportion to Asia.[1] And, of course, medieval mapmakers made sure to indicate the dangerous waters leading to unknown territories where "thar be dragons!"—signaled by detailed illustrations of dragons, sea monsters, and other mythical creatures who stood for those locales we know are somewhere around the bend but whose inhabitants we do not know or understand.

"Mappa Mundi"

A medieval mappa mundi, then, marked not national boundaries or natural terrains, but rather spiritual and psychosocial ones—worldviews, we would call them today. They told stories about how people imagined the world and themselves in it.

While we've come to make maps with greater geographical accuracy, we fool ourselves still if we believe that our modern maps reflect any uncomplicated, uncontroversial reality. This is because the nations and the borders we now recognize through the boundaries drawn on modern maps are political *ideas* rather than geographical facts, the results of negotiated histories and relationships. Ask the people of Tibet where China *really* is (or vice versa), and you'll come into a swirl of contested history, tradition, and politics. As the saying goes, what you see really does depend on where you stand. Likewise, of course, the lines of longitude and latitude found on some maps don't exist in any physical form. They merely mark a system of vertical and horizontal coordinates used to identify the precise location of any area on the earth for the purposes of navigation and geographical identification.

Though it may be the case that it is far easier to navigate across the globe with a modern, geopolitical map, it is no less the case that such maps also chart a modern worldview, which assumes the idea of separate nation-states and global navigation along gridlines that make the globe into manageable quadrants. Indeed, most modern maps make the assumption that few of us will travel by foot or otherwise on the ground, generally eliminating the challenges of mountains, lakes, and rivers as other than properties of this nation or that state.

This is no less true in maps of the evolving digital world, where social networking sites have allowed people to cross all sorts of boundaries, setting aside traditional and/or political notions of nation, ethnicity, class, ideology, and so on—including religion. Hence China's tight control of social networking participation that could—would likely, if we read the 2011 revolution in Egypt through this lens—introduce ideas into the culture that might challenge or override the official narrative. While China holds a remarkable advantage in terms of global capital and geographically located population, a new mapping of the world that highlights the population of just the Facebook social networking community tells a very different story.

The dark areas on the map below are where Facebook is the dominant digital social network. Outside of Brazil, where Google's Orkut social network dominates, the areas not covered by Facebook are often the territories of more repressive regimes in which the networked, relational, sharing and co-creating of new knowledge is seen by government leaders as a threat. The remarkable fact is that if the population of people who participate on Facebook across the globe were a nation, that country would be the third most populous—just behind China and India, and having more than twice the population of the United States. What's more, if territory where Facebook dominates were ceded to this new digital nation, it would have as much land mass as North and South America combined, with Africa thrown in for good measure, making it the largest continental territory in the world.[2]

Map of the Facebook World

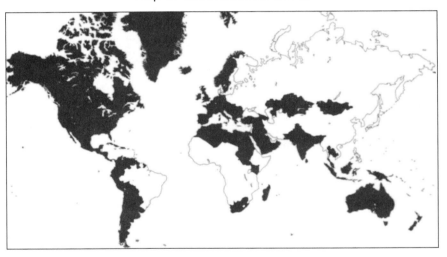

Of course, Facebook doesn't exist geopolitically (yet), but a map of the world drawn on the basis of social media participation surely opens a whole new worldview—one in which modern constructions of national identity that are often tied to religious identity are thrown into flux. This blurring of boundaries that for generations we believed were fixed spills out of the online world into physical reality, were people increasingly question cultural constructions of things like gender, race, sexual identity, class, social status, and vocation. We live in a world that is now characterized by the confluence of ideas, collaboration among those separated by time and distance, and the convergence of written, visual, and auditory media across a less and less ideologically and geopolitically partitioned global landscape.

What this means at a minimum is that, despite our local, sometimes parochial, orientations, we always conduct our ministries in a global context that extends far beyond the expanse of the Christian colonializing impulse of the eighteenth and nineteenth centuries—certainly well beyond the doors of our increasingly empty churches. What's more, the political and economic power that funded Christian colonialism has shifted in the new digital world order, giving *everyone* with access to a computer, a laptop, or a lowly smartphone the opportunity to enter, reshape, and even dominate conversations about faith in everyday life. Thus, whether or not we choose to bring our ministries actively into the world reshaped by social media, citizens of that world always have the opportunity to draw us into it by sharing commentary, images, and other content about us and our churches or organizations.

CROWDSOURCING CHRISTIANITY

Now, this could mean that we engage social media defensively—finding ways to ferret out negative perceptions of our leaders, denominations, churches, and other organizations. Indeed, a cottage industry of sorts has grown up around this kind of "reputation management," serving mainly corporations, politicians, and celebrities by searching for and attempting to erase negative comments, reviews, images, and the like. But this isn't the only way, nor, we would argue, the best way, to engage the new, digitally widened world. We see digitally connected global networks as profound opportunities to reverse

CROWDSOURCING

Crowdsourcing, the idea of outsourcing to an unknown group of responders, is the practice of using social networking to draw upon the expertise and/or resources of people distributed across the globe to solve a problem or address an issue.

Christian parochialism and colonialism by enabling us to more fully enter into conversation, relationship, and common action that doesn't override the gifts of one culture with those of another, but which gathers the best of all of us into the Christian project of kingdom-making.

JAMES ROLLINS
Director of Marketing and Communications, United Methodist Committee on Relief

 The challenge of sharing information on the United Methodist Committee on Relief's and Methodist Global Ministry's efforts on behalf of the church is not a small one. Neither is encouraging people to support projects that address the spread of malaria in Africa, the creation of community health programs in the Philippines, or the engagement of youth and young adults in service projects in their communities and across the globe.

Rising to such challenges is all in a day's work for James Rollins, who sees social media not merely as a faster, less expensive conduit for messages to the faithful. He sees social networks like Facebook, which serves as a hub for a variety of online UMCOR ministries, as centers of engagement and participation within and across communities.

The UMCOR "10-Fold" project, for instance, is an online event that begins

Continued

In a sense, as James Rollins describes the social media ministry of the United Methodist Church, this makes every church a global relief agency, every congregant an active agent of God's love and compassion in the wider world. This work is no longer the narrow purview of church-sponsored NGOs, who collect money from churches to distribute around the globe on behalf of believers.

In the digital world, this gathering of globally distributed participants in loosely organized communities is called "crowdsourcing," a practice that ignores the traditional boundaries of geography, status, gender, race, class, and so on to draw on the practical wisdom of everyone with an interest in helping to solve a problem, disseminate ideas, or collaborate on projects related to shared interests. Crowdsourcing is now used to support the microfinancing of small businesses around the globe whose owners would never qualify for traditional financing (as through the microlending sites Kiva and MicroPlace). But it's more often not so focused and goal-directed. When you participate in social media networks like Facebook, Twitter, LinkedIn, and the like as someone who is open and articulate about her or his faith, you are, in effect, crowdsourcing Christianity, crowdsourcing the church. You are extending the love of Christ both within and beyond the boundaries of your local community and, more than that, inviting others to share their faith and their lives with you and your community.

Whether or not this translates into more "pledging units," you are vastly expanding the reach of the faith in the world.

RELIGION RULES FACEBOOK

That's just the tip of the iceberg. The average American Facebook user spends about twelve minutes a day checking in on her Facebook news feed, updating her status, and "liking" or commenting on friends' statuses. Slight though this may seem, it adds up to more than five hours a month on Facebook alone.[3] Users in Israel and Russia spend twice that amount of time, clocking more than ten hours a month on Facebook.[4]

There's more! By summer's end, while you were relaxing in your hammock, the Jesus Daily Facebook page was ranked the number one "most engaging" page, trouncing teen heartthrob Justin Bieber and soccer powerhouse Manchester United.[5] The Jesus Daily page was hardly alone at the top as a marker of the religious interests of Facebook Nation. Also in the top twenty were pages for the Bible, Jesus Christ (one of many), "Dios Es Bueno!," "I'm a Muslim & Proud!," and Joyce Meyer Ministries. Eleven of these came in ahead of Barack Obama and glam-pop megastar Lady Gaga.

Importantly, the "most engaging" ratings are not based just on the number of members a Facebook page has—Bieber and Gaga are well ahead in terms of raw numbers. Rather, the ranking takes into account the number of interactions

JAMES ROLLINS *Continued*

on October 10 each year (10–10). For ten days, ten projects around the world are highlighted through webcasts, streaming video, and online chats that put people in local church communities in conversation with people in communities where Global Ministries and UMCOR projects are unfolding.

"This is way more than a fundraising or even an awareness-raising effort," explains Rollins. "The 10-Fold project is an experience. It allows everyone in the church to have the actual experience of seeing and listening to the people we serve. It absolutely creates a global community for the ministries we do."

Though 10-Fold has a separate website (10-fold.org), Rollins stresses that the success of the 10-Fold project, which was recognized by the Religion Communicators Council as "Best of Class" in 2010, is very much dependent on a robust Facebook network. "Facebook is the starting point for much of our communication," says Rollins, "because that's where people already are. It amplifies and, in a way

Continued

maybe, bypasses traditional church communications. We are able to be in touch with people whether or not they happened to be in church on Sunday. And, it also starts a conversation that people will take into our churches on Sunday."

Rollins notes that the remarkably interactive 40,000 members of the UMCOR Facebook page are not just gathering information on and discussing UMCOR-sponsored projects. They're also sharing their own service. So, for example, you'll see a request for a local campaign to educate people on human trafficking on All Saints Day to be extended across the wider Methodist Church community. You'll find discussions of what sorts of snacks to put in backpacks for low-income kids who might not have enough food over the weekend. Folks share photos of bags for relief supplies and instructions on how to sew them. And, of course, there's lots of prayer, praise, and thanksgiving.

"What's important here," says Rollins, "is that all of this media belongs to everyone. We're all creating it and sharing it together."

on the page, including posts, comments on posts, and likes. What has pulled religion-oriented pages to the top is not, then, that people of faith are interested only in displaying their faith, but that they also want to talk about it with others.

This engagement factor highlights a key aspect of digital ministry that we noted in the introduction and that bears repeating here: ministry in the Digital Reformation—not only in digital locales but also in local spaces in which interaction is increasingly shaped by digital practice—is networked and relational rather than broadcast and numerical. It's about how you connect in meaningful, personal ways with people across diverse networks, not about *how many* people hear your message. It is here that, we feel strongly, approaches to ministry online based on commercial marketing strategies are bound to fail miserably in the long run. People don't want to buy what you're selling. They want to know who you are.

Before we move on to learn more about who all these religiously engaged social media participants are, take a moment to consider this: What would it mean to your church or other faith organization to have an active cohort of people who, even for five minutes a day, were interested in gathering to pray, comment on scripture, discuss the needs of the world in light of their faith? If those folks were willing to gather outside your doors, would you be willing, as a ministry leader, to take time to encourage them and help to enrich their time together?

Well, these folks might not be outside your office door, but they are certainly right outside your digital door, on Facebook, Twitter, LinkedIn, and more. Indeed, the Pew Internet & American Life Project reports that a full 65 percent of American adults who use the Internet are members of Facebook, MySpace, or LinkedIn—participation that has doubled since 2008 and is increasing at a rate of about 10 percent per year.

WHO INHABITS THE DIGITAL WORLD?

Generically speaking, the typical social media user looks something like this:

LIKING

"Liking" on Facebook is when you click the word "like" under a post, photo, or video. This causes a teeny thumbs up icon to appear below the post:

🖒 You like this.

"Liking" is a quick way to show you're paying attention, give a nod of approval, or just say "hello" on someone else's Facebook wall. It makes minimal, but often meaningful, engagement possible within your Facebook community.

See Chapter 3 for more on using Facebook in digital ministry.

Typical U.S. Social Networking Participant[6]

Blacks (69%), Hispanics (66%), and Whites (63%) participate at comparable levels in social media sites.

People with Less than a High School Education (68%) and people with a College Degree (67%) are most likely to be social networking site members.

People from Urban (67%) and Suburban (65%) areas are slightly more likely to participate in social media communities than people from Rural (61%) areas.

69% of women belong to social networking sites compared to 60% of men.

Among the top social media cities: San Francisco; San Jose, CA; New York; Austin, TX; Minneapolis-St. Paul; Seattle; Boston; Raleigh, NC.

49% of people access social media through mobile phones. **Users who access via mobile divice are twice as active.

Globally, social networking participation skews more toward men, a trend which is echoed among participants in the largest social network, Facebook:

Typical Facebook Participant[7]

Connects to 80 group pages

20.6% are age 13–17.
25.8% are age 18–25.
26.1% are age 26–34.
14.9% are age 35–44.
8.0% are age 45–54.
4.6% are age 55–64.*
* fastest growing segment

Spends 15.5 hours per month on Facebook; 23 mins. for each visit

Has 130 Facebook Friends; interacts regularly with 20 of them.

Globally, 51.2% Male; 48.8% Female.
In the U.S., 54.3% Female; 45.7% Male.

70% of Americans with internet access have a Facebook profile.
95% of South Africans with Internet access have a Facebook profile.
100% of Columbians and Venezuelans with internet access have a Facebook profile.

Twitter is used far less than Facebook. Twitter itself reported some 100 million active users in the second half of 2011, but there have been significant questions about how active most of those users really are.[8] Still, Twitter's growth has been strong, with more than three hundred thousand people joining each day. Its growth has been amped up by its role as a conduit for on-the-scene reporting after natural disasters in Haiti and Japan and political uprisings in the Middle East. Beyond the urgent or otherwise newsworthy, the site has proved to be a valuable resource for researchers tracking the more general public mood,[9] which makes aggregated Twitter feeds a gold mine for understanding how people feel about politics, economics, and other important issues—like, oh, faith, spirituality, religion—on a daily basis.

Its 140-character format is particularly attractive to mobile phone users, making it a more accessible platform for social networking in regions where more expensive desktop, laptop, and tablet computers are thin on the ground. Outside of the U.S., Twitter is most popular in the Netherlands, Japan, Brazil,

Indonesia, and Venezuela.[10] Based on data from the Pew Internet & American Life Project, a typical American Twitter participant looks something like this:

Typical U.S. Twitter Participant[11]

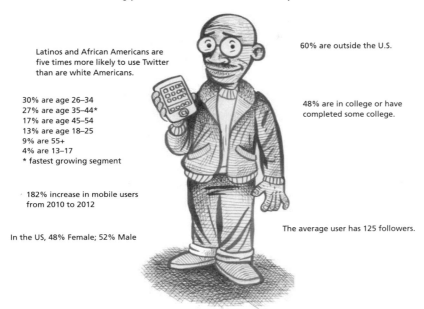

Latinos and African Americans are five times more likely to use Twitter than are white Americans.

30% are age 26–34
27% are age 35–44*
17% are age 45–54
13% are age 18–25
9% are 55+
4% are 13–17
* fastest growing segment

182% increase in mobile users from 2010 to 2012

In the US, 48% Female; 52% Male

60% are outside the U.S.

48% are in college or have completed some college.

The average user has 125 followers.

In Chapter 3, we will provide some further notes on the characteristics of the users of other social media platforms, but this overview of users of the two largest platforms and of social networking sites in general should help make clear that the people most absent from many mainline communities—those under age fifty, men, and people of color—are most likely present in social networking communities. And they are far from uninterested in religious or spiritual concerns.

DIGITAL MINISTRY STRATEGY

When we look at the profile of typical Facebook or Twitter users in light of our most immediate communities and those we most hope to engage, important questions are raised about how we map the world from our particular perspectives. From where you sit, what is the center of the universe, toward which the bulk of your interest, energy, and time gravitates? To what extent does that gravitational pull prevent you from engaging the needs of the wider world in your ministry? How would you mark the borders between your world and the worlds outside your door? Where would "thar be dragons"—areas of real or imagined danger that seem off limits in your community—and how do they stand between your ministry and those it would more richly serve?

The worksheets that follow are meant to help you think about what your world looks like from the inside out and, perhaps a bit more, from the outside in, since we've found that the best social media strategy is one that starts with an assessment of where you are right now. We've also shared a community social media assessment that will help you to better determine the resources and expertise you will be able to bring to your digital ministry and the skills you will want to develop as you move forward. Take some time, then, on your own or in small groups in your community, to think through the worksheets that follow as the basis for a fuller social media strategy.

PART I: MAPPING YOUR WORLD

As we've discussed, a map is both conceptual and spatial. It tells at least as much about how people see the world at any given time as it does about the reality of towns and cities or roads and the rivers they cross. People serving churches and religious organizations carry certain maps of the world in their heads as much as anyone else does, and these maps subtly guide the way we approach and practice our ministries.

For example, Elizabeth led members of a church communications committee through a workshop exploring the challenge of engaging people shaped by digital culture. They began by thinking about the *mappa mundi* within which their church tended to operate.

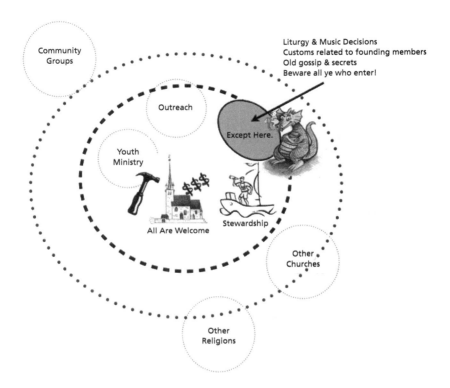

They noticed that, although their belief and the church's mission put Christian witness at the center of their world, in fact, the challenge of keeping up the building was really, as one group member said, "our Jerusalem." Everything revolved around dealing with the physical property, which hardly allowed them to reach out to those outside the church without a fairly transparent agenda to snag them as pledging members. Moreover, it meant that boundaries between the church and other community organizations were fairly inflexible, as few in the committee had time to take up work that might turn them away from member-seeking and fund-raising. However much they claimed to want to engage young adults and encourage greater diversity in their community, they had mapped their world in such a way as to set such people far beyond their borders, in mysterious, unexplored lands where creatures with which they could not imagine contending might roam.

Working together to sketch their map of the world helped them to see their reality more clearly. It also gave them the opportunity to identify places where they might build bridges, crack a window open a bit, or invite new kinds of networked, relational engagement. Of course, this did not just apply to digital ministry, but extended into their local ministry practice as well.

The first step, in both locales, is having a clearer sense of your own *mappa mundi* as it shapes ministry practice. From there, you can move on to consider who lives within your world and with whom you might like to connect and what borders you would need to cross. Use the guidelines below to develop a *mappa mundi* for your community, then go on to develop a fuller profile of yourself and your community members.

Your Mappa Mundi

Using a large sheet of flipchart or butcher paper, draw a map of the world from the perspective of your ministry or those of your faith community. The key below offers some icons that will help you to mark out the territory in which you minister, but be sure to develop your own images to fill out your view of the world.

Solid Border—No one crosses without proper documentation

• • • • • • • • • • • • • • • • •

Porous border—People can cross, but they still know they're in your territory when they enter

NO TRESSPASSING

Where is it just not okay—physically, theologically, or otherwise—for the uninitiated to go?

Thar Be Dragons!

Where in your world is it made particularly clear that people are welcome?

Where is it clear that you connect with the world outside?

Step 2

Complete this step after completing the following three worksheets.

How are different individuals and groups located in your world?

PART 2: YOUR SOCIAL MEDIA PROFILE

Before you begin to explore social media platforms that might become sites for digital ministry, take some time to assess yourself as a social media participant.

Age

❏ 18 to 24 ❏ 25 to 35 ❏ 36 to 45 ❏ 46 to 55 ❏ 56 to 65 ❏ Over 65

Education Level

❏ High School ❏ Some College ❏ College Degree
❏ Graduate Degree ❏ Other: _____

Location

❏ City/Town ❏ Suburb ❏ Country

Social Media Participation

In which of the following social networking sites do you participate and to what extent?

	A lot	Some	A little	Not at all
❏ Facebook	❏	❏	❏	❏
❏ Twitter	❏	❏	❏	❏
❏ YouTube	❏	❏	❏	❏
❏ LinkedIn	❏	❏	❏	❏
❏ Foursquare	❏	❏	❏	❏
❏ Blogs	❏	❏	❏	❏
❏ Other: _____	❏	❏	❏	❏

Your Typical Church or Religious Organization Member

Now, you should assess the social media profile of your ministry. The Community Social Media Ministry Survey on the next page will help; consider sharing it with people in your ministry.

COMMUNITY SOCIAL MEDIA MINISTRY SURVEY

Social networking sites like Facebook and Twitter have become incredibly popular among almost every age group and demographic cluster. And, religion and spirituality are among the hottest topics in social networking communities. As we begin to consider how our ministry might engage this new terrain, we'd like to know about your experience with social media.

Your Age Group
❑ Under 13 ❑ 14 to 17 ❑ 18 to 24 ❑ 25 to 35
❑ 36 to 45 ❑ 46 to 55 ❑ 56 to 65 ❑ Over 65

Your Education Level
❑ High School ❑ Some College ❑ College Degree
❑ Graduate Degree ❑ Other: _____

Your Location
❑ City/Town ❑ Suburb ❑ Country

Your Social Media Participation
Which of the following social networking sites do you use and how much?

	A lot	Some	A little	Not at all
❑ Facebook	❑	❑	❑	❑
❑ Twitter	❑	❑	❑	❑
❑ YouTube	❑	❑	❑	❑
❑ LinkedIn	❑	❑	❑	❑
❑ Foursquare	❑	❑	❑	❑
❑ Blogs	❑	❑	❑	❑
❑ Other: _____	❑	❑	❑	❑

Would you be interested in helping to develop a digital ministry strategy for our church or organization?
　　　❑ YES ❑ NO ❑ Tell Me More

Would you be interested in participating on a digital ministry team?
　　　❑ YES ❑ NO ❑ Tell Me More

Your Name: _____ Email Address: _____

Once you've got a reasonable portrait of your community and yourself, place yourself on your world map in relation to typical Facebook and Twitter users. Where will you need to build bridges to connect more fully with people in your own community and to invite those outside into conversation with you? In the chapters that follow, we'll look at very specific practices that will help you to do this, but it's important to know early on where the opportunities and challenges lie. Looking in from the outside, how would typical social media users see you and your community of faith?

Average Age in Your Community

❑ Under 13 ❑ 14 to 17 ❑ 18 to 24 ❑ 25 to 35
❑ 36 to 45 ❑ 46 to 55 ❑ 56 to 65 ❑ Over 65

Average Education Level in Your Community

❑ High School ❑ Some College ❑ College Degree
❑ Graduate Degree ❑ Other: _____

Where Most People in Your Community Live

❑ City/Town ❑ Suburb ❑ Country

Social Media Participation

In which of the following social networking sites do members of your community participate and to what extent?

	A lot	Some	A little	Not at all
❑ Facebook	❑	❑	❑	❑
❑ Twitter	❑	❑	❑	❑
❑ YouTube	❑	❑	❑	❑
❑ LinkedIn	❑	❑	❑	❑
❑ Foursquare	❑	❑	❑	❑
❑ Blogs	❑	❑	❑	❑
❑ Other: _____	❑	❑	❑	❑

2

THE REAL PRESENCE
Developing a Unique, Authentic Voice
for Digital Ministry

There are two essential elements to successful personal digital ministry: presence and voice. Our presence as digital ministers should be compassionate, engaged, inspiring, accessible, and informative, but above all it must be real. It must be an authentic representation of ourselves as real human beings and as ministers. The cultivation of a distinct voice helps to distinguish us among the cacophony of voices in social media communities. In this chapter, we will describe what this "real presence" looks like and share examples of ministry leaders and congregations that are bringing a well-defined presence and distinctive voice to bear in their ministry.

KEITH RECEIVED SOME SAGE ADVICE before beginning parish ministry. That wisdom applies to digital ministry:

I had just been ordained as a pastor and called to my first congregation. The responsibility of that office was weighing heavily on me, and I wondered whether I was up for the job. One evening, I shared my worry with my good friend, Knute, who gave me some of the best advice I've ever received about being a pastor, before or since: "Keith, people just want a pastor who's down to earth, that they know cares about them."

Of course, I knew that. I had heard and experienced that truth in countless ways throughout my preparation for ministry. However, in my anxiety about being responsible for a parish full of souls, I was overwhelmed with all that I had to do and be to fulfill the pastoral office. Not surprisingly, I had completely overcomplicated the matter. Knute's advice called me back to a simple truth about ministry: hokey as it may sound, we are most effective when we are down-to-earth, real people—when we are ourselves. In the midst of my anxiety, I could hold on to that. I could do that.

Many people feel anxious about embarking on the journey into digital ministry. Doing ministry in the digital media landscape described in the previous chapter feels to many like a new kind of call in a strange new land—one with different patterns of behavior, relationships, etiquette, and modes of communication that require us to develop new skill sets. It can be both exhilarating and disorienting.

With all the tools now available to us, and with the responsibility of being a minister in a new unfamiliar digital space—one in which many parishioners or community members are more advanced than we are—we worry about whether we can manage it all. In our anxiety—before we even jump in—we may debate the proper boundaries about friending people from our church, how many profiles we should have, how much time to spend (all of which we will discuss later in this chapter). Most of the time, we focus on *the terms of engagement* rather than actually *engaging* with members, friends, and our community.

Knute's advice is salient here: "People just want a pastor who's down to earth, that they know cares about them." In whichever way you choose to participate in digital media, and with however much time you commit, this has to be at the center of your digital ministry.

"Keeping it real" in this way is both good pastoral practice and the most effective way to engage people in digital social media locales.

"FRIENDING"

"Friending" is the practice of inviting people into your network on Facebook. The noun became a verb as people accepted requests and asked others to be Facebook friends.

"Friending" has joined the common lectionary beyond Facebook, especially among teens and young adults, who now often "friend" one another face-to-face as folk from "the days of yore" would speak of "making friends."

See Chapter 3 for more on using Facebook in digital ministry.

KEEPING IT REAL

The word most often used—and perhaps overused—to describe this kind of real presence in social media is "authenticity." It's been argued that authenticity is a term that is impossible to define. Like "beauty" or "truth," we tend to know it when we see it.

In *The Gifts of Imperfection*, researcher, storyteller, and social media practitioner Brené Brown describes authenticity in this helpful way:

> Authenticity is a collection of choices that we have to make every day. It's about the choice to show up and be real. The choice to be honest. The choice to let our true selves be seen. There are people who consciously practice being authentic, there are people who don't, and there are the rest of us who are authentic on some days and not so authentic on other days.[1]

According to Brown, authenticity is about showing up with our whole selves. The work of ministry continually calls us to "consciously practice being authentic." Life experiences, passions, strengths, and weaknesses are all brought to bear and shape pastoral presence, regardless of whether we are serving as clergy or laypeople. Being true to these—and trusting that God is at work in them—is what makes each ministry unique and effective. It enables us to empathize with people in their suffering, bring the Word of God home in preaching and teaching, and share faith through the stories of our lived experience.

The same goes for life and ministry enacted through digital media. Our real presence is essential. By bringing the fullness of our lives to bear through ministry in social media communities, we bear witness to the fullness of life in God. After all, the *really* Real Presence here is God's, and it is through our real and authentic presence in social media that we most clearly and effectively point to God. As we know from face-to-face ministry, this is often how faith is transmitted and God is made manifest: through the stories of the real lives of real people.

Let's take a closer look at what real presence looks like in the context of social networking.

IT'S SOCIAL, NOT BROADCAST, MEDIA

In the five hundred or so years between the inventions of the printing press and the Internet, we have lived in a broadcast media environment of books, radio, newspapers, and television. These media served as highly effective platforms for sending a single, well-crafted, attention-getting message out to as many people as possible. But broadcast media afforded little opportunity for feedback, except, perhaps, for letters to the editor. In the church, we have used this one-to-many broadcast communication model in sermons, printed newsletters, letters from the pastor, and broadcasting worship services on the radio or local television community access channels.

Social media represents a profound shift in this model. Today, almost anyone can publish a blog, have a YouTube channel, and host their own internet radio station. Anyone can comment on, extend, qualify, discuss, and share your sermons. As we will discuss in the next chapter, now even small congregations can have a robust media platform.

Rather than waiting for your monthly newsletter, now people can and want to follow you on Twitter. They can "like" your organization's Facebook page and follow your church ministries in real time. They can "friend" and "follow" other members. They can chat, message, mention, and "tag" you. They can help generate content and conversation by posting on your organization's Facebook wall.

TAGS AND HASHTAGS

 A tag is a word or very short phrase that describes people or content of interest to online users. It helps to make information online searchable by people with similar interests.

Individual blog posts will tend to have set of tags—keywords—that describe the contents of the post. For example, the tags *church, ministry, social media, Facebook, Keith Anderson* might mark a post about a workshop Keith's done on digital ministry.

In addition to helping others to find content and understand its main themes, tagging can be an expression of identity—a sort of digital tattoo—that names what's important to a particular social media participant.

On Twitter, tags are marked with the # symbol, so you will find people who end each tweet with a denominational tag like #ELCA (for Lutherans) or #TEC (the Episcopal church) to signal the spiritual identity of the tweeter regardless of content. This is called a hashtag.

These dramatic changes necessarily shape our message, presence, voice, and practice of ministry. However, because this broadcast model has been so pervasive, most people first approach social media as simply another form of broadcast media—as one more way to blast our message out there and get people to join our church or organization. This approach to social media is bound to fail. First, because the emphasis is on the needs of the institution rather than

"FOLLOWING"

 "Following" is how people connect on Twitter. Unlike on Facebook, where you must request access to another user's profile by "friending," on Twitter you can access almost any user's tweets by clicking the "follow" button on a user's profile:

 **Follow**

Only if a user follows you back can you use Twitter features like private messaging, but, as you'll see in Chapter 3, there are lots of other ways to connect on Twitter.

the needs of the individual. It's about *our* message. Second, because people want and expect to engage with you personally. They don't just want information. They want and expect to have a relationship.

IT'S CARING, NOT SELLING

In his book *The Thank You Economy*, Gary Vaynerchuk describes this shift from broadcast to social media by drawing upon an important distinction between *caring* and *selling*.

Vaynerchuk tells the story of how he helped grow his traditional family-owned wine shop, Wine Library, through an active digital social media presence. The story begins with Twitter.

Vaynerchuk began by following conversations on Twitter about wine, specifically chardonnay, and answering questions and giving recommendations. But he made a point never to link to his own website. He wanted to make a human connection, not just a sale. He writes:

 To find conversations on particular topics on Twitter, enter a term at *twitter.com/search* and the latest tweets with that keyword will appear:

For example, you can look for your denomination or more general terms like "spirituality," "prayer," "Christianity," and so on.

Eventually, people started to see my comments and think, "Oh, hey, it's that Vaynerchuk guy; he knows Chardonnay. Oh cool, he does a wine show—let's take a look. Hey, he's funny. I like him; I trust him. And check it out: he sells wine, too. Free shipping? Let's try a bottle of that. . . ." That's what caring first, not selling first, looks like, and that's how I built my brand.

Now, at the end the day, Vaynerchuk does want to sell something.

He wants people to order some wine. And he knows that engaged and happy customers make for good revenue streams and, thus, profits. In some respects, it is not about relationships themselves, but about monetizing relationships. In business, relationships are typically a means to an end. This is certainly not necessarily evil. People need and want lots of things, and it is more pleasant to go about obtaining these things from people

Occasionally review your list of friends on Facebook or followers on Twitter as a reminder of who you are speaking to when you post.

who are able to connect with you on a personal level, who are attending to something of your authentic self. For digital ministers, however, the meaningful relationships we create and nurture should be ends in themselves, not the means to increasing our membership or giving levels.

This is a subtle but quite powerful distinction that often makes much of the very good advice on using social media for business marketing not particularly adaptable to church settings. We are ministers, not marketers, so our presence in digital spaces must be very clearly defined in terms of authentic ministry—an authentic connection with others that focuses on the sharing of love, wisdom, and gifts rather than monetary or other transactional exchanges.

That said, Vaynerchuk is right about this: people need to know that you care—and they need to care about you before they will ever care about your institution. They must be invested in your mission and ministry before they will be invested in the success of your congregation or organization in achieving that mission. Being human, authentic, and caring is the entry point for engagement with you and your congregation.

So, don't just share information about your church. Don't sell your church or yourself. Move beyond "creating buzz" by promoting others, making connections, making introductions, encouraging others, and sharing your story, experiences, and life of faith. Perhaps most importantly, telling your church's story should always be preceded by

Part of being personal is not trying to speak to everybody at once. This often happens naturally, but try to address small groups among your friends and followers. Your tone will be personal, but it allows others to overhear.

sharing your story. In social media, the personal is primary. As Elizabeth has argued, "Institutions don't do social. People do social."[2]

People want to connect with people. That's the whole point of social media. Effective social media ministry invites and nurtures these personal connections.

IT'S PERSONAL, NOT INSTITUTIONAL

The Lutheran Church of the Redeemer, which Keith pastors, has evolved a more personal, relational digital ministry over time. They first came to social media in 2006 when Keith began posting the manuscript of his weekly sermons on a blog. This was mostly for his own use. It was an easy way to categorize, archive, share, and search sermons.

Two years later, just as Facebook was becoming popular, the church council established four strategic goals for the congregation. One of those goals was improving church communications. A small group spearheaded the effort. Keith built a new church website and Redeemer pushed further into social media, creating a Facebook page, Twitter feed, and using iTunes, YouTube, Constant Contact emails, and multiple blogs to share not only sermons, but podcasts, adult education programs, and the latest congregational news. Over these last three years, Keith and the congregation have used just about every type of social media available. Altogether, they have provided a robust platform to connect with people within and beyond the congregation and share God's grace. Like many of the people and ministries profiled in this book, Redeemer's experience with social media has been one of thoughtful experimentation. Some of the brightest ideas—like a blog with resources for nurturing spirituality—have petered out, and some things started on a whim—like a 2-Minute Bible Study on YouTube you'll hear more about in Chapter 3—have surprised with how strongly they resonated.

The most important lesson in digital ministry is that people want to connect personally. Thus, although you are a priest, pastor, or other minister, and use social media in your ministry, the content you share should not be just about church or faith. Keith, for instance, shares updates about family life, his passions for web design, running, social media. And, he increasingly uses the social geolocation platform Foursquare, which we'll describe in Chapter 3, to check in and tell a story about where he is and what he's doing both as a pastor and as a human being in the world more generally. Elizabeth, on the other hand, tends to share updates about political and artistic interests, about life in Northern California, and, of course, about her dog—a gracefully aging Akita named Maya—along with gleanings from her research, teaching, writing, and involvement in the Episcopal Diocese of El Camino Réal.

Sharing your story and your passions, being present and active in social media, humanizes you. This is a great gift for ministers, parishioners, seekers, and other conversation partners. People learn about what a clergyperson or a lay minister does during the week, but they also learn that a ministry leader is a person with a life beyond church. These other interests also provide easier points of entry and encourage more dynamic connection than you'd get with a link to your sermon blog or church events calendar.

You can often share the exact same content on your church Facebook page and your profile; you're likely to get more "likes" and comments on the profile. That's because people know that you're going to see it personally, and that you will likely respond to them personally. This just feels better than getting what seems like a generic note from an anonymous administrator.

But it's not just about you. We both generate a fair amount of religious content through the week: blog posts and a video from Keith, articles and interviews from Elizabeth. But we also share the work of others. We link to other posts, tag and mention people—friends, colleagues, and parishioners. We give plenty of shout-outs by liking, commenting, and sharing on Facebook, and retweeting and mentioning others on Twitter.

Dan Zarrella, a social media analyst, summarizes it this way: the best way to approach social media participation is to "stop talking about yourself. . . . But start talking *as* yourself and show us how the world looks through your eyes."[3]

MINISTRY OF DIGITAL PRESENCE

Social media communities are no longer just places to keep up with family and friends. They are a place where we keep up with a diversity of relationships, interests, and commitments.

People keep up with news, organizations, teams, friends all in one place. As a result, our personal and professional lives are integrated across a single Facebook wall and, for more and more people, supplemented by a Twitter stream. This phenomenon is called social convergence, which, as Presbyterian minister, blogger, and mission developer of Project FM (more in Chapter 4)

THE REVEREND JODI BJORNSTAD HOUGE
Humble Walk Lutheran Church

 Humble Walk Lutheran Church is a congregation that intentionally worships and meets in public spaces in the West End neighborhood of St. Paul, Minnesota. Founding pastor Jodi Houge describes herself as a "prolific poster" on Facebook. She says, "Since I don't have an office or physical structure, it is the place where I am most present. People know where to find me. It's either by Facebook, email, or text. It's all technology-based and I would have never dreamed that would be my most consistent presence as a pastor. But it really is how it happened and how it continues to happen."

People know Pastor Houge is present by virtue of her high level of activity. She uses her digital presence to point to her physical location as she encourages people to drop by the coffee shop for Bible study or the pub for theological conversation.

Adam J. Copeland explains, "occurs when different social contexts are brought together into one."[4] In this way, our Facebook walls both reflect and shape our lives.

Ministers of all sorts have longed to be a more integrated part of people's lives and not just segregated to Sunday morning. Now we have that opportunity. The advent of new digital media gives us an unprecedented ability to tell our personal and congregational stories—and God's story. Everyday, perhaps several times a day (for the average user on Facebook, nearly fifteen minutes a day),[5] people are scrolling through news, pictures, comments. We can appear as a visible reminder of their church community, their faith, and God's grace.

Digital ministers are like chaplains walking the halls of the hospital, or a parish priest walking the streets of the neighborhood, at times offering a smile, a wave, small talk, a prayer, or deeper conversation. Our presence here makes us available to others—and points beyond ourselves to the presence of God. This digital ministry presence can unfold in the same way that wearing a clerical collar around town is a way of saying God is here and there is something worthwhile and, yes, holy about this place.

It also makes us available and accessible. David Hansen, the pastor of St. John Lutheran Church of Prairie Hill in the small town of Brenham, Texas, is a fourth-generation Lutheran pastor. He reflects, "I remember my dad walking around with a beeper and a bag phone in the late '80s so people could reach him. Because, for him, before people can have a personal interaction with you, they have to reach you first. It is all about connection. Ministry is about being part of people's lives." Today, his father, who is semi-retired, logs in to Facebook on his iPad.

As Hansen suggests, we can't be just empty profiles. There must be someone at the other end of the line—or profile. We can't just create an account and expect people to engage with us. We can't automate all our posts or have someone do it for us. Our presence must be demonstrably active and authentically us.

The more present you are and the more you participate, the more people will engage with you. People generally interact with you according to the level of your activity. If you're not active on Facebook—if you have few friends and don't post much—people won't even try to contact you for fear you won't see it. They will get in touch with you by email or phone—or, perhaps, not at all. Today, that is an extra step many people are not willing to take.

FINDING YOUR VOICE

There are billions of voices across the digital landscape, and it's natural to wonder what impact a parish pastor, youth minister, diocesan staff member, or lay minister can actually have.

SISTER HEATHER ROLLINS, OPA
Undercover Nun

 Sister Heather Rollins, a sister in the order of Anglican Dominicans, took a very different approach to finding her digital ministry voice. She originally began tweeting and blogging under the pseudonym of "Undercover Nun," playing "a nun in plain clothes." On her blog (*undercovernun. net*), despite the motto, "I'm not always in my full habit," Rollins was more open about her vocation. Over time, her secret identity was revealed to her rector and the master of her order, and her distinctive spiritual voice became clearer across media platforms.

Rollins gives this advice: "For somebody who's getting started it helps to find some kind of hook that's special to you. For me, it was that Undercover Nun, having that sort of outlook, saying things you'd expect a Catholic nun school teacher to say. That made it easier for me to find content to talk about and to have conversation because it just got responses. It helps when you find something that's part of you and focus on that on first, and it will broaden over time. Find whatever your little special niche is and what you're passionate about and go with that."

The key to distinguishing yourself among the many people within social media is to find your own unique voice.

Of course, you already have a voice—you already have something to say or else you wouldn't be in ministry. One of the reasons ministers are well suited to social media is that they regularly create content and specialize in relationships, and to do that they have honed a distinctive voice. Every week you bring your unique perspective and lens on the Gospel to bear on the world. Thus, the challenge is not necessarily to create a new voice, but to translate your voice and perspective from your ministry into social media.

Generally speaking, a strong social media presence that best articulates a clear and distinctive voice is consistent, positive (even when critical), diverse in its interests, passionate, plain-spoken, humorous, focused on others, responsive, uses mixed media, does not take itself too seriously, is not self-promoting, and highlights unique qualities of the minister and of her or his ministry.

While every voice will necessarily be unique, we have tended to see the presence of digital ministers fall into seven categories:

Activist—provides content on social justice issues, shares their own activity, and asks people to take action

Affirming—is more active on other people's pages than their own, offering likes and comments

Informational—provides links to local or national news and other content in areas of particular interest

Pastoral—offers prayers and blessings, expressions of concern and support for members of a more defined (congregational, denominational, organizational) ministry community

Educational—shares educational content on topics of interest to themselves and others

Social—enjoys interacting with many people across platforms, connects social media users to one another, and shares personal content that helps to deepen connections

Spiritual—shares prayers, spiritual quotes, inspirational images, and music; prays for the needs of individuals and the world

Your digital ministry will very likely often fall into multiple categories, but it can be helpful as you're starting out to focus your participation in one primary category. If you're working with, for example, a church communication or outreach team, you might want to distribute responsibilities for engagement across the categories above. This is important—and it's important to refocus your personal digital ministry in other categories if you see that you're most consistently operating out of one—because different social media participants are drawn to different kinds of content and interaction.

Once you've entered the digital world as a recognizable, authentic ministry presence with a clear and engaging voice, there are a number of other ministry practices common to face-to-face ministry that you will have to adapt in your social media participation.

MANAGING DIGITAL TIME

Many ministry leaders see social media as an add-on to their already full ministry schedule, one that they simply don't have time for. It's just "one more thing" in an already over-booked schedule.

We're all aware that technology and social media can quickly consume our time. It's no wonder much of the conversation among lay and ordained ministers about social media revolves around how to maintain limits on the amount of time they spend in social media. Indeed, the first message Keith received on his Facebook wall was from one of his parishioners, Eric Dewar, who greeted him saying, "Welcome to the vortex. Facebook is the biggest time-suck ever."

It can be, certainly. But it doesn't have to be. Setting limits is important for both the novice and those already highly engaged in social media. If you're new at social networking, it's a good idea to commit yourself to an amount of time, at least twenty minutes each day, to log in, read, and respond. As you get more proficient, you will make increasingly better use of that time and you may want to do more. But you don't have to. As Christian spirituality author Margaret Benefiel, who stays in touch with nearly two thousand Facebook friends, notes, "I can connect in basic, meaningful ways—'liking' something on someone's profile or saying 'Happy Birthday'—in about fifteen minutes in the morning or over a couple five-minute breaks in my day. I've made a choice to be present, but it's not an obsession."

THE REVEREND CLINT SCHENKLOTH
Good Shepherd Lutheran Church

 Clint Schenkloth, the pastor at Good Shepherd Lutheran Church in Fayetteville, Arkansas, and the creator of the ELCA Clergy Facebook group (which boasts over three thousand members), describes his basic philosophy on social media as "No Distinctions." He says, "It's not like I've got a separate pastor thing and a separate Clint thing and a separate hobby thing. I am who I am, which includes being a pastor and maybe a hobbyist on a couple different things. So my public persona is kind of the same everywhere, on my blog or on Facebook or Twitter, whatever." For safety reasons, he says very little about his family. "I don't tend to publish names of my children and I'm careful what I say about my spouse."

It may feel easier to say little, or to create a highly filtered social media presence. Schenkloth disagrees: "If I don't want my youth group to see me

Continued

DIGITAL SABBATH-TAKING

If you spend a great deal of time online, consider taking time to unplug and provide for a social media sabbath—a designated period of time each week when you shut down all your social media sites. Likewise, you'll do well to set some boundaries on social media on your days off, just as you'd set on how frequently you retrieve phone messages or email. Don't post about or respond to church business on these days, and make a note in your status bar or on your wall so people know "The Minister Is Not In Today." If you use the Facebook chat feature, set your status to "offline."

MAINTAINING BOUNDARIES

The flip side of the unprecedented access that social convergence gives us to the lives of those to whom we minister is the unprecedented access it gives people to ours. It collapses the barriers we have been taught to raise between our private and public, personal and pastoral lives. This has created anxiety around social media for many in ministry.

Boundaries are absolutely necessary in ministry for a host of reasons, not least of all to manage power dynamics, safeguard relationships, protect the vulnerable, and avoid emotional and physical burnout. So where do we draw the line in social networking communities?

As in face-to-face ministry, the boundaries will be different for everyone, varying by style, personality, and context. It seems unwise and unhelpful to mandate a particular approach for everyone. For many years, the bright uncrossable line was not to befriend parishioners personally, because it might compromise our ability to be their minister. As the Reverend Kelly Fryer argues, this may have been more myth than reality, even before the dawn of social media.[6] Fryer explains:

THE REVEREND CLINT SCHENKLOTH *Continued*

post this on Facebook, does anyone want to see it posted on Facebook? Is it healthy for it to be there anyway? I tend to try to let being completely public be the thing that keeps me from posting anything that would be actually inappropriate to anyone."

When I was graduating from seminary, the second most unhelpful piece of advice I received was "Don't make friends with parishioners." The idea was that you were supposed to keep up a professional distance from the members of your congregation in order to . . . what? I'm not sure. Avoid congregational infighting over who gets to be friends with the pastor? Maybe if we were all in fifth grade.

This already fuzzy concept of not becoming friends with those whom we serve in ministry is further confused because the term "friend" itself has been transformed by Facebook. A "friend" can range from a confidant to a casual acquaintance to someone you've never met. To mitigate this aspect of social convergence, some have created separate ministry and personal accounts, effectively partitioning their online presence. They use ministry profiles for relating to parishioners and their personal profile for friends. However, they miss out on the benefits of sharing their faith with friends and their life with their parishioners. And, as Schenkloth's approach highlights, the pastoral role is about sharing the Gospel, building community, nurturing relationships, and doing outreach. In many ways, then, social media platforms and the convergence they create are a healthy corrective to the partitioning of our lives. For, just as damage can be done when we blur the pastoral and personal, we can also do damage when we cut ourselves off from different parts of ourselves.

Pastor Jodi Bjornstad Houge of Humble Walk Lutheran Church says of this division between the pastoral and personal, "I just found that to be impossible because it's all interwoven. . . . I recognized right away that because of this call that I have to Word and sacrament, there is no way to separate 'clergy Jodi' from everything else. And so everything that I put out in social media is still holding a public office. Much of it is just me and my life, but it's always public."

Many of the digital ministers we've met tell us that the practice of setting up two accounts is less about cutting themselves off from parishioners and more about wanting to preserve the fun of social media and freely connect with friends. There is a sense of loss of the freedom that others have to share personally and speak your mind. "Look, once in a while I'm going to want to cuss or to say that your favorite political candidate is an idiot," said a church communicator who maintains two Facebook profiles and separate Twitter feeds (and who asked not to be named). "Yes, I want people in my diocese to see me as a whole person who has a life beyond my ministry in the church, but I don't need for everyone to see me in my bathrobe, or with a lampshade on my head on New Year's Eve, or whatever."

And yet, this is simply another way in which digital ministry is like face-to-face ministry. Wherever we are, with whomever we are with, we represent the church. We represent the church whether we are on a personal or professional profile, a page or group, whether we have lampshades on our heads or are sipping tea with a circle of kindly church ladies. Using social media in ministry—using social media at all—requires thoughtfulness and discretion. Below, you'll see some ideas about how this works.

BEING A SHEPHERD, NOT A SHEEP

In place of a clichéd "don't be friends with parishioners" rule, a helpful rule of thumb offered by the Reverend Nadia Bolz-Weber of House for All Sinners and Saints (whom we profile in Chapter 4) is "don't try to get your emotional needs met by them." Don't try to make your friends, followers, and readers into your personal chaplains and spiritual guides, calling on them to shepherd you through the ups and downs of your life.

Says Bolz-Weber, "My main thing is that I try to never put up any status update that seems emotionally fishing. My parishioners should not feel like they have to take care of me emotionally. I have personal friends for that."

Now, this is not necessarily the same as asking for prayers, admitting that you're having a bad day, sharing a life event, or declaring that you think your sermon sucks. Those things can, in fact, make us human, approachable, and real—and people often respond with great wisdom, compassion, and humor to such posts. But when we post we have to ask ourselves: "Why am I posting this? What am I looking for? Sympathy? Attention? Intimacy? To fill a deeper need?"

For example, sometime back, Elizabeth was a bit taken aback by a Facebook post from a clergy member who was clearly way too in the thick of it while holding her iPhone in her hand to make particularly clear judgments. "I'm not sure what I like best from my male colleagues," she posted sarcastically, "the condescension or the belittling."

She apparently rallied in a matter of seconds, for the post was deleted almost immediately, and it's likely that few of her flock saw what was probably some measure of legitimate frustration but also a skewering of some of her colleagues that was undoubtedly inappropriate for a public setting like Facebook. Even in the few seconds the comment was up, a number of people did comment on the post, offering a level of "there, there, dear" consolation and "you give 'em what-for!" encouragement that ministers don't usually want to be soliciting from their flock en masse. And, one male friend gently suggested that jerks come in all shapes, sizes, and genders.

PERSONAL, NOT PRIVATE

A more helpful distinction than *the personal and the professional* is perhaps *the personal and the private*.

Darleen Pryds, a professor at Franciscan School of Theology in Berkeley, California, and an advocate for integrating social media into education, likens her experience of social media to her experience of living, for a while, next door to the school where she taught:

> I was very close and I would walk my dog and students would come up to me and ask me about assignments and stuff, so I had to put clear boundaries on that. So what I did unselfconsciously at first, but then consciously, was to talk about my dog. That would become the one area that was safe and everyone would talk to me about my dog. My dog, Gracie, became a kind of star. In that regard, I became much more public about one area of my life and then I really put the boundary on everything else in my personal life. Facebook is the same way. I post just enough to keep my students interested in me as a person, but certainly I don't tell everybody everything.

Recently a person in my Facebook network went on something of a rant over an article I posted related to the alienation young adults feel from the church, particularly in relationship to baby boomer leadership. The reader's comments grew into an increasingly irate diatribe about "whiny, spoilt, privileged children." Others felt obligated to intervene and balance the conversation. Finally, I sent the friend, whom I knew from a church community, a private message:

> I know you're new to the Facebook community, so I think you're maybe not aware of some of its norms. First, you've probably noticed that people leave relatively short comments—maybe a sentence or two—rather than long treatises. This tends to let other people into the conversation, which functions more like a cocktail party or coffee house chat than like a seminar or lecture series.
>
> Also, at least on my wall, I like to maintain a certain level of civility even as we're discussing things about which we have strong feelings. I expect people to

Continued

In Keith's parish work, he actively friends parishioners. He wants to be their pastor in digital space as well as in face-to-face settings. It is another way for them to communicate and for their pastor to be available. And, especially in light of the worries many have about ethical behavior online, a digital minister can serve as a good example of participation in social media communities with an ethic of kindness and compassion.

RESPONDING TO BAD BEHAVIOR

Boundaries run both ways. What if one of your friends or followers is behaving badly or not observing social media etiquette? What if someone is posting inappropriate content and/or posting excessively or too personally on your wall?

It's your wall, your blog, and your Twitter stream. You have the right to remove anything you deem inappropriate. You can delete individual posts or block certain users from posting. You can create customized rules on Facebook that prevent specified friends from seeing all of your posts.

However, we encourage you to try to approach these as opportunities for conversation and modeling appropriate social media behavior. First, send the person a direct message explaining your concern. If, however, the bad behavior continues, we recommend responding with "progressive discipline," deleting posts from people who over-post or who post inappropriately.

While we've both had to do it once or twice, we feel that unfriend-ing someone on Facebook or block-ing them from your Twitter feed should be an absolute last resort for people in ministry. We want to be in relationship even with—maybe sometimes especially with—people who can be challenging or outright difficult. Part of the promise of church in social media communities is that we can stay connected, even when we disagree. We do this face-to-face with difficult people in our congregations all the time.

It may turn out, however, that with some challenging people, a social networking site is not the right context for ministry, not just because it exposes you and your online com-munity to various difficulties, but because it also exposes the offender to everyone's digital gaze. If you ran into a parishioner having a breakdown in the grocery store, odds are you'd do your best to get him or her to a more private space so you could better attend to the matter at hand. So, too, your more intimate online ministry may sometimes move well offline.

The cases in which we always recommend drawing a firm line by unfriending or blocking someone—and communicating privately that you are doing this—are when there is bullying toward you or any other member of your network, when there is pronounced religious, political, or ideological hostility toward other's views, or when someone seems otherwise unable to adhere to very basic norms of respect for others and discretion in the ideas, photos, videos, and other content they share.

> **Continued**
>
> avoid name-calling and profanity, and to generally show respect for the opinions of others, even when they disagree. It seems pretty clear that the article I posted pushed a button or two for you, and I do care about what you think. But I also care about the other people in my network who may have taken umbrage at both the tone and the length of your posts. I know I did. I hope I can ask you to moderate your tone in future conversations and allow space for other people to participate.
>
> In this case, the problematic par-ticipant not only desisted, but also apologized to the participants in the conversation.

There's a lot to think about here, and the worksheet that follows will help you to consider how you want to shape your own digital ministry presence and that of your church or organization. In the next chapter, we'll explore each of the dominant social networking platforms—blogs, Facebook, Twitter, YouTube, FourSquare—and what they offer to leaders in ministry in much greater depth. As you prepare for that part of the journey, we return to the wisdom of Pastor Clint Schenkloth: "Think of what you're doing in social media *as* ministry, not commentary on it, not ancillary to it."

DIGITAL MINISTRY STRATEGY: REAL PRESENCE

The following questions are designed to help you better articulate your "real presence" in social networking communities. Reflect on them for you personally and, either on your own or with a group, in the context of your ministry community.

1. Using the categories we described for digital ministry presence, note where you see yourself as most comfortable now and what might be a growth area for you. How might you develop in your growth areas? You might want to complete this assessment for both yourself and for your church or organization.

	Comfort Zone?	Growth Area?	How do you engage OR How could you grow in this area?
Activist	❏	❏	_____
Affirming	❏	❏	_____
Informational	❏	❏	_____
Pastoral	❏	❏	_____
Educational	❏	❏	_____
Social	❏	❏	_____
Spiritual	❏	❏	_____

2. Look through your Facebook friends, the groups you like, and the people you follow on Twitter. Who would you identify as your social media role models, both as individuals and organizations? What makes them particularly engaging for you?

Who?	Why?
_____	_____
_____	_____
_____	_____
_____	_____

3. What are some personal-but-not-private things you can share to human-ize your presence in social networking communities? What forms do these things take (e.g., tags, photos, stories, quotes)?

_____   _____

_____   _____

_____   _____

_____   _____

3

I LOVE TO TELL THE STORY
Social Media Platforms

 Social media, with its facilitation of easy many-to-many communication, has shifted the Internet from a warehouse of information to a place for storytelling and connection. Your intentional presence and engaging voice are the basis for sharing a compelling narrative about your life and ministry that unfolds over time in text, pictures, videos, check-ins, blog posts, and tweets, inviting people into conversation and relationship.

Choosing which social media platforms to use in your ministry will depend on the kind of story you wish to tell, how you wish to tell it, and to whom. In this chapter, then, we will explore the major social media platforms that form the core of an integrated digital ministry practice: Facebook, Twitter, LinkedIn, blogs, YouTube, and Foursquare.

SOME TIME AGO, Keith experienced how telling an engaging story well online brings you into relationship with others, often before you even know them:

 I was the last to speak.

I was attending a ministry workshop led by Christian spirituality scholar Margaret Benefiel on understanding personal and congregational change. We were going around the circle, making the customary introductions. The introductions had begun on the other side of the room. Ministry colleagues, mostly from the United Church of Christ, Methodist, and Catholic traditions, introduced themselves. Finally, when it was my turn, I said, "I'm Keith Anderson and I'm the pastor at the Lutheran Church of the Redeemer in Woburn." Before I could say anything more, someone blurted out, "Are you *that* Keith Anderson?"

I had no idea if I was or not. My mind raced. "Do I know this person?" I wondered. "Wait, am I in trouble?"

I need not have panicked. "Didn't you write some article—something about welcoming people into your church?" my fellow participant asked. Indeed I had. I was *"that* Keith Anderson."

A couple months earlier, I had posted "Top Ten Things We've Learned About Welcoming Newcomers" on my personal blog. I shared what we'd learned in our efforts over the last five years in our work to become a more welcoming congregation. I posted a link to the post on my Facebook profile. There, it came to the attention of a seminary classmate, who, in turn, recommended it to the Lewis Center for Leadership at Wesley Seminary in Washington, D.C. The piece was later included in the Lewis Center's *Leading Ideas* e-newsletter, to which many of the colleagues at this workshop subscribe.

And so, before I uttered a word beyond my name and congregation, there was a story being told about me and my congregation—by people far beyond our geographical location or denominational tradition.

My colleagues and I chatted briefly about the post, and the conversation continued during the breaks. When the workshop was over and we all returned home, a story that began in social media continued in the same way as we friended one another on Facebook.

Keith's story illustrates an important lesson: if you are participating in social media communities, in any capacity, you are already telling a story about yourself and your congregation, consciously or not—a story that has the potential at any moment to extend well beyond your local and social media communities. Think about this in terms of the demographics of Facebook we discussed in Chapter 1, for instance. There, we learned that the average Facebook member has about 130 friends, and is in regular contact with only about twenty of them. But the "only" there is misleading, because those twenty friends connect to another twenty friends and so on, and so on. The network of your potential influence through social media is exponentially larger than the network of people with whom you're connected or you interact directly. As in Keith's story, you have no idea where the content you share will end up and how it might impact your ministry.

At least as importantly, if you're not yet participating in social media communities, you are also already telling a story by virtue of the absence of your engagement, and your church's, with the wider world as it is mapped today. Today, before anyone walks through your church doors or meets you in person, she or he is constructing a story, developing a picture, and forming a preliminary relationship with you and your congregation through what you share (or don't) online. When you are not present in online communities, you're passively telling a story about you and your church's or organization's disinterest in where people spend much of their time—more than five hours a month. You're saying, "Hey eight hundred million people in Facebook Land, we're not really interested in you!" That's probably not the story you intend to tell.

But by being present and active in social media platforms, we can help shape—not control, but shape—our personal and community stories and the relationships they encourage. This takes wise use of social networking platforms and practices.

CHECKING IN ON THE ROAD TO EMMAUS

Just as Biblical writers employed different genres—letters, poems, songs, gospels, narrative, and myths—to tell the story of God and God's people, we can use different social media platforms and tools to develop our distinctive stories in engaging and nuanced ways. The type of social media we deploy depends on what kind of story we are trying to tell and to whom.

Stories shared in social media networks can be driven by location and movement, as in the Gospels, which feature Jesus' own "check-ins" from Nazareth to Jerusalem. We can use location-based social media like Foursquare to tell our own pilgrimage stories. We can share evocative imagery akin to the Psalms in poetic tweets on Twitter and with more literal images of the sort that adorn the stained glass windows in many of our churches through photo sharing with applications like Twitpic for Twitter or on our Facebook profiles and pages. Versions of our epistles can now be blogged or captured on video and shared on YouTube.

There are, of course, many other social media platforms at your disposal, including MySpace, Flickr, and most recently, Google+. All of these services

CHECK-IN

A social media "check-in" lets people in your network know where you are at any given moment. Platforms like Foursquare use GPS tracking to tell your community exactly where you are. Facebook apps for mobile phones and tablets also include a check-in app. So, your Facebook page will have a post like this:

Gretchen Weller Mertes was with Ian at Luther's Table.
Like · Comment · October 11 at 11:59am via mobile · 🏢
👍 Bill A likes this.
💬 View all 4 comments

See more on Foursquare check-ins in section 3.6.

will evolve and will eventually be eclipsed. Indeed, this is a common argument for waiting to engage in social media. However, most new technologies will be built on the ones we use now, so the guidance in this book is designed to be generally adaptable to any social media platform you choose.

For example, the design of Google+ is based on Facebook. Google+ adopts the Facebook status update, the concept of gathering friends and colleagues (which Google+ calls "circles"), and adds more refined features and utilities like "hangouts," where up to ten users can have video chats. You really don't need to know all the detailed ins and outs of Google+ to use this new platform once you understand the basics of Facebook or Twitter. Whatever social media comes next will likely draw on similar features.

SEWING UP YOUR STORY

In any story, some basic elements must be present: a plot, characters, dialogue, and, most of the time, movement from place to place, scene to scene. These all serve to create something not simply informative, but something experiential, as when we read a good book and sink into the reality it evokes. Good stories invite the reader to participate, enriching the stories through their imaginations and—in the social storytelling that connects the Digital Age directly to the Middle Ages—in conversations as the story unfolds in the presence of others.

Biblical narratives were frequently compiled from the work of more than one author—a poem or song stitched together with a parable and a bit of a local legend to tell the bigger Truth of God's presence among us. This stitching has left visible seams, frayed edges, and gaps within the biblical text. The uneven stitching enriches the biblical story, revealing a multitude of meanings, understandings, and interpretations, and inviting new perspectives into the divine-human narrative. So, too, the patchwork of content and conversation—the overlapping and interwoven voices—in social media spaces can offer great richness and depth.

In fact, it is really only by stepping back and attending to the full relational, conversational tapestry of social media that we are able to see beyond the common argument that life online is necessarily "shallow" or "impersonal." Take a bit here, a byte there, a pixel or two over yonder, multiplied by relationship upon relationship upon relationship across a vast, global matrix of networks, and you come to find considerable depth and substance. "Aggregate depth" is the term Elizabeth has used to describe this gradual, little bit by little bit, approach to developing richer relationships one status update or one 140-character tweet at a time.[1]

The stories we share—and ask people to enter, shape, and share again—form the overarching narrative of God's redeeming grace. Despite protests to the contrary, in a distributed, digital way, this makes our social media participation profoundly incarnational. Anytime you have someone say, "Oh, I saw this article posted on Facebook today . . ." in a face-to-face conversation, you're getting a glimpse of the incarnational potential of social media particapation.

NOW DEPARTING FROM THE PLATFORM

Note that the term "platform" is used in two different ways when talking about social media. Each type of medium—Facebook, Twitter, blogs—is a platform in the sense of being a digital locale in which people can interact around shared interests. Facebook is a place, a location. Thus, you'll hear friends and parishioners say things like, "Oh, I saw you on Facebook yesterday."

The second meaning is more like a political platform: not a specific locale, but rather how you engage across a combination of these sites to connect with others and develop relationships. Your participation on a combination of social media platforms helps you to articulate your ministry philosophy and approach—your ministry platform—and engage with others.

With social media, an effective ministry platform is developed by integrating all the social media locales into a consistent, recognizable online presence. Your ministry does not begin and end when you speak from the pulpit. It's also comprised of pastoral care, religious education, and so on. So, too, your digital ministry is multifaceted. It unfolds across multiple, coordinated social media platforms. Together, they construct your digital ministry platform.

In the era of broadcast media, the most influential ministry platforms tended to be those of large congregations with equally large budgets, synod committees, diocesan programs, staff functions, seminary professorships, or people who had the opportunity to write for magazines and newspapers. The number of these positions was already limited, and had been commonly reserved for senior ordained clergy. Now, as mainline denominational structures shrink, these traditional opportunities and platforms are becoming more scarce—and less influential. Meanwhile, today, with just a blog, Facebook profile, and Twitter feed, you can influence conversation in the church just as much or more than those in traditional leading roles. You can have a disproportionately large influence within your denomination, community, and congregation. (That's how a parish pastor from eastern Massachusetts wound up writing this book with a professor from northern California.)

Even small congregations can have a robust presence and influence in the new media landscape. Take Pastor Nadia Bolz-Weber's congregation, House for All Sinners and Saints (HFASS), which we'll profile in detail at the end of the book. Begun in 2008 as a mission start of the Evangelical Lutheran Church in America (ELCA), House for All Sinners and Saints lacks all the traditional media platforms, yet its ministry is highly influential. Congregations around the country incorporate some of their signature events, such as Beer and Hymns, Blessing of the Bicycles, and Theology Pubs, in their own ministries. While these practices did not originate with HFASS, they have become identified with the community (at least in the ELCA) precisely because of Bolz-Weber's active social ministry presence.

Certainly, lots of other communities have developed and practice innovative and engaging ministries. But the influence such ministries have earned HFASS in the wider church has, according to Bolz-Weber, everything to do with how social media has allowed them to be part of a widely distributed narrative of the church and its ministries:

> Our church is very well known for being such a small church. Our average worship attendance is seventy people. But we do have a big presence. It's helped us make our case for why the ELCA should keep supporting us. We're

like, "You're not just helping pay for a pastor for less than a hundred people. You're helping provide this laboratory where we get to experiment with stuff and publish our results, which has been really useful for people serving other churches that aren't laboratories."

Before exploring how you and your congregation can develop your own integrated platform for digital ministry, be aware that some of the most important things we do through social media are on other people's platforms. We can respond to others' posts by commenting, "liking," sharing on Facebook, retweeting and mentioning on Twitter, and leaving blog comments. It is possible to have a meaningful presence without managing your own particular platform. Your initial strategy may be to respond to the content and activity of others. Even once you are up and running, it's a good practice to spend more time on other people's platforms than your own.

In the rest of the chapter, we will overview the main features of each of the major platforms: Facebook, Twitter, LinkedIn, YouTube, blogs, Foursquare. We'll also take a glance at Google+. Each section features a summary of different levels of experience with the platform using what should be familiar religious categories: Novice (beginner), Oblate (initiated member), Superior (expert). At the end of the chapter, you'll have the opportunity to reflect on how each of these platforms might fit into your digital ministry and how you plan to approach growth in your digital ministry expertise on each platform.

3.1 FACEBOOK

Number of Users	750 million worldwide as of June 2011; 70% outside of the United States
Typical User	In the U.S., female, between the ages of 26–35 See Chapter 1 for more details
Key Features	• Personal profile • Personal and institutional pages • Groups • Posting of status updates, photos, links to other content, videos, chat
Benefits of Participation	Almost everyone who uses social media is on Facebook
Limitations	Annoying advertising
Cost	Free, though paid services are in the works and paid advertising is available.
Similar Platforms	• Google+ • Bebo (Especially in Latin America) • MySpace (Though membership has declined significantly. Core market is teens and independent bands promoting their music.)

THE BASICS

Facebook enables you to tell a media-rich story to the largest number of people across generations—from tweens to grandparents. It is the social networking platform that people use the most (upwards of fifteen minutes a day) and understand best.

Facebook is excellent for:

- Sharing a variety of content: pictures, videos, music, links, text
- Sharing links to content from other content sources, such as blogs and YouTube
- Promoting and coordinating events
- Connecting with parishioners, across generational lines
- Leveraging existing contacts—most Facebook friends are already friends (or friends of friends) offline
- Communicating with and responding to others, either publicly or privately

Digital ministry novices and those with limited time should take Facebook as a starting point. With so many people present, and multiple forms of content, you get the most mileage for your time. Plan on spending about an hour to set up your profile, and invest about fifteen minutes a couple times a week—really, that's all—to get going.

Facebook is also a great environment for learning the multimedia ropes of the social networking landscape more generally. Through Facebook, you can share not just a personal or community profile and regular status updates, but also pictures, videos, music, longer notes, and geolocation check-ins. The process for adding such content on other social networking sites is basically the same.

NEWS FEED

 The Facebook News Feed is the stream of status updates, links, photos, and comments from people and organizations in your network. These stories are automatically organized by Facebook into "Top Stories" (based on some mysterious Facebook algorithm), but you can select "Most Recent" from the top of the News Feed page.

Remember, however, that there are millions of people not on Facebook or who are also active elsewhere—often more than they are on Facebook. For example, many business professionals prefer LinkedIn (see section 3.3 below), a business networking site that focuses on professional networking and career development. Sometimes employers discourage employees from using Facebook in any substantive way, but most allow participation on LinkedIn. So, once you build competence on Facebook, you'll want to venture further into other platforms, even if only periodically.

Within Facebook there are three venues for telling your story: your personal profile or timeline, pages, and groups. We'll start with the profile, but many of the practices we discuss are also applicable to Facebook pages and groups.

FACEBOOK PROFILE

Your personal profile or timeline (which we'll get to shortly) is the backbone of your Facebook presence. Your profile is your digital identity in the Facebook community, sharing not just your name, birthday, location, and professional status, but a full range of perspectives on your life as these are revealed in photos, favorite quotes, interests, political views, and the often vexing category of "religious views." Your Facebook profile allows people you already know to find you, and invites those with similar interests or friends in common to connect to you and to each other.

A quick look at United Church of Christ pastor Kim Hinrichs's profile shows a warm and smiling California transplant to Lincoln, Nebraska, whose life extends from ministry to family to vibrant gatherings at an Omaha sushi restaurant. Hinrichs uses videos from her church, and of her daughter's inspired back stoop musical performances as well as photos of the family lounging at home or zipping around the go-cart race track, and links to spiritual and political content to round out the profile of a vibrant, reflective, active ministry leader. A recent video, which Hinrichs introduced by posting, "This is what I do on Sundays," shares her offering an awe-inspiring rendition of prayers of the people with a soulful rendition of "Come, Bring Your Burdens to God" offered in the background by the First Plymouth UCC choir.

This portrait is so much richer and more dynamic than any church website could be because it's updated much more regularly—several times a week to several times a day. People see Hinrichs as a minister, a mother, a spouse, a friend, and a community member because they get an ongoing glimpse of her everyday life:

FACEBOOK TIMELINE

In 2011, Facebook introduced a "timeline" feature that presents your pro-file information in a highly graphic, magazine-style format. The timeline format aims to evoke the personal and human by offering a graphically enhanced picture of your interests and activity. It amplifies the visual over the textual, a rebalancing of image and word that is particularly important in digital culture.[2]

Timeline gives you two options for posting: subscriptions and lists. When you activate subscriptions, anyone on Facebook can follow and view any updates that you designate as "public." You may want to make some of your posts "public" to allow people who are not yet friends to get a sense of what you're interested in and to encourage them to engage with you.

Facebook automatically organizes your friends into smart lists like "Fam-ily," "Close Friends," or people who attended the same school. You can edit these lists, adding or deleting friends from your wider network. You can also create your own custom lists, like all members from your parish, colleagues, and people in your local community. Depending on your content, you may wish to post to a particular list, so that you're sharing, for example, your great joy over Stanford's defeat of Notre Dame (or, okay, most likely vice versa) with your college friends.

Facebook lists allow you to organize your networks into smaller affinity groupings, which enables you to focus posts to specific clusters of friends.

But take care not to over-filter. Even though all of your churchy friends might not be into your football interests, your comments on other aspects of your life nonetheless create a fuller portrait of who you are, allowing people to see you as more than a narrowly pastoral figure.

WHO IS MY FRIEND?

Everyone who requests to be in your Facebook network and is accepted, and everyone who accepts your request to join their network, is your "friend," regardless of their status in your personal life. When you join Facebook, you will be prompted to allow Facebook to connect with your email address book so that you can see who in your existing network is already on Facebook and send invitation emails to those who are not. You can also use the Facebook Friend Finder by typing the name of a person or organization in the search bar. This will connect you not only to individuals, but also to Facebook groups and pages where people with common interests gather. You will probably want to look for Facebook groups related to your denomination, for example, or to specific ministry interests.

You also have the opportunity to connect, even loosely, with key figures in your denomination, the Church more broadly, or in other areas of interest. Facebook profiles for luminaries such as Desmond Tutu or Pope Benedict are, in effect, personalized

TAGGING ON FACEBOOK

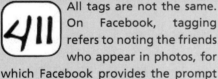 All tags are not the same. On Facebook, tagging refers to noting the friends who appear in photos, for which Facebook provides the prompt "Tag this Photo" when you or another user clicks on a photo on your profile page or in a News Feed.

It also applies to naming friends in your status updates or posts. When you start to type a name, Facebook will automatically prompt you to include the full name, which links to the profile.

Continued

institutional pages. But some pretty cool folks actually maintain an actively engaged personal presence on Facebook. The scholar and writer Parker Palmer, for instance, poses questions on his Facebook page as he's reflecting on new ideas or fleshing out writing projects, and he participates in conversations that may play out over days on Facebook. The spirituality writer Barbara Brown Taylor is seldom active on her page, but her fans often are, creating a wide spiritual community. These sorts of connections won't likely be the center of your Facebook network, of course, but you may enjoy keeping up with some of the individuals and organizations you admire most. And, such connections share more depth on who you are with other friends in your network.

The bulk of your personal network will be people you already know, and you'll want to start out by

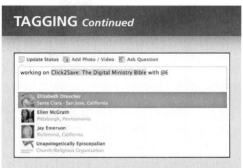

TAGGING *Continued*

Tagging photos and posts gives you greater connection within your network as well as to the networks of the friends you name. When you tag someone, the post or photo appears in the news feeds of people in their network as well as those in yours.

However, everyone doesn't love this feature, either universally or for a specific photo or post. You or a friend can remove tags, or set privacy settings not to permit them. When a friend removes a tag, be respectful of their choice by not naming or tagging them in future posts without asking for permission.

"friending" as many of them as you can so you're quickly in conversation. It's worth making a note in your church's or organization's newsletter that you've joined Facebook and are interested in connecting with members of the community. When you are on your profile page, the address bar in your Internet browser will have your unique Facebook address. You can share that in your announcement and invitation.

There will likely be more friends in your personal network than your church's Facebook page will have fans. Your profile will also reach beyond your church constituency to include family, friends, and acquaintances, who are already interested in what you're up to because they know and care about you. Here, you don't need to discuss every church activity. Signature events are probably sufficient, with links to your church's Facebook page.

THE DIGITAL WORLD HAS GONE TO THE DOGS (AND CATS)

On your personal Facebook profile, people get to know you as a person, outside of the ministry context. Expect more response here rather than on your church page. People like interacting with other people much more than they do with institutions.

Ministry leaders often worry about how much personal information to include, especially with regard to their children or partners. Here, take a cue from Diana Butler Bass, Nadia Bolz-Weber, and other well-known ministry leaders and thought leaders who, on the one hand, want to establish meaningful relationships in social media settings and who, on the other, want to keep their personal lives relatively private: talk about your dog. This allows you to share content that is personal, but less private than information about your family, your vacations, and the like.

Diane Bowers, the pastor of St. James Lutheran Church in San Leandro, California, has sustained a vibrant, interactive conversation about a stray cat, Nina, that she cared for over the summer. She's posted tales of Nina's adven-

tures getting from the back porch to the cozy laundry room and videos of her exploits as the temporary First Cat of Bowers's household.

Bowers uses another very effective approach to sharing personal information that steers away from the private: she talks about books she's reading, generating conversation among members of her congregation and her wider circle of friends who've read the same titles or who have other suggestions for her.

Last winter, Keith's family adopted a golden retriever puppy named Charlie. He posted videos of little Charlie climbing the snow banks outside the Anderson house. His social networks responded with a collective "Aaawww." It was an important event in the family's life, which felt authentic and personal to share and had the effect of humanizing Keith and connecting at a personal level (after all, who doesn't love puppies?), without splashing pictures of his children or much of their home all over his Facebook wall.

THE MORE THE MERRIER DIGITAL MINISTRY

Extend your ministry's Facebook presence by encouraging other staff members to share your work together on Facebook. This helps spread your story to their social networks, and confronts the assumption that it's all about the pastor, priest, or minister. You can have some fun with it and interact with one another in an open conversation people can see. Friends you have in common will see the information multiple times, and everyone will have a fuller sense of all the people—lay and ordained—necessary to make a faith community functional.

Beau Surratt, the music minister in two Episcopal congregations in Chicago, is a primary social media voice for the communities he serves, sharing his life and ministry on both Facebook and Twitter. His social media ministry extends his own everyday spirituality into the wider digital world, but it also speaks, formally or not, for the churches with which he is affiliated. Everyone in your congregation or on the church staff with a Facebook page or Twitter feed does exactly the same thing when she or he posts about something going on at church, about ecclesial or diocesan issues, theological concerns, and so on.

Actively inviting a wider community into a social media conversation about faith and their participation in your church or organization makes the public story about your community more multidimensional. And, it allows you, as a ministry leader, to stay connected to how your community tells that story.

What's more, information shared on profiles has the weight of a friend's recommendation, which is the most influential form of word-of-mouth. Thus, one of the most powerful things you can do is have members of your congregation share your content. As we discussed in Chapter 1, the average Facebook user has approximately 130 contacts. If ten people share, say, a link to your church website, it will be seen by as many as 1,300 people in their news feed—maybe more.

PRIVACY

Privacy on Facebook and other social media platforms is not just about how you manage what you actively share. It also requires paying attention to the privacy settings on each platform. Even as we were writing this book, Facebook privacy settings were changed and may have changed since this printing. On Facebook, privacy preferences located in the account settings

If you set up a Facebook page or group for your church or organization, make sure to use your personal status update to ask people to "like" the page. This will get the word out that your community has crossed the digital divide.

pulldown menu determine who will see your content.

Even before the subscriptions feature was added, allowing Facebook users not in your network to view posts you designate as public, Keith made many of his posts public. When someone links to his profile page they can actually see some of the content and get a better feel for who he is and the topics he's interested in. Now, with subscriptions, people can follow those posts whether or not they are a Facebook friend. It's a good idea, then, to make a few public posts that lots more people can see. For that matter, make some of your information (like work and education) public so people can determine whether or not to friend you or accept your friend request.

No matter your privacy settings, be aware that once you post something on Facebook or any other social network, it is public. People can copy and paste, if they wish, or refer to it on Facebook or another social network. So, even if you limit the extent to which you distribute information, photos, and the like, you can't assume anything about how people in your network manage their privacy settings.

For instance, when Keith went on a youth mission trip to Pittsburgh, he decided not to post on Twitter, where updates are completely public. He wanted to avoid publicly revealing that he was away from home for a week, so he posted about the trip on Facebook to his friends instead. Then, a colleague noted on Twitter that he hadn't seen Keith on Twitter lately and wondered where he'd been. A mutual friend, who had seen his posts on Facebook, said Keith was in western Pennsylvania on a youth trip. His cover was blown. The lesson: networks are fluid and overlapping. You cannot control how your content is used once you put it out there. It can be as simple as a cut and paste or as innocent as a Facebook friend who follows you on Twitter asking how your trip is going.

FACEBOOK PAGE

Facebook pages function as extensions of church or organizational webpages—ones which can be more easily updated. Anyone can see or join your page, so the emphasis tends to be on your external audience. People only need to click the "Like" button at the top of the page to like and follow you. After that, your updates show up in their News Feed. Following a page is easy, and rather passive. You'll want to generate interest and activity through your posts. Make sure to maintain visual interest by including photos, videos, and links along with textual updates.

If you intend to share the same piece of content on both your ministry page and your personal profile, it's a good idea to post on your ministry page first. From there, share it to your profile. A link to your ministry page will appear along with the content you are sharing. This, in essence, double-dips your personal network and your page's network.

By default, fans of your ministry page can post on it. You can adjust permission settings if needed. You probably don't need to post more than three times a week to keep the page current, but a daily post—even a short quote or a photo from your community archives—will help to keep the page vital and dynamic.

Keep in mind that your page may be the only spiritual resource people engage in their work-a-day lives. While social media engagement ideally leads to face-to-face relationships, this doesn't always happen. For some, a Facebook page is a spiritual end in itself. So, it's important to be sure your posts are not all about driving people to your webpage or through the church doors. Providing inspiration right there on the page is an important part of your ministry. Indeed, this spiritual element of the Facebook experience is undoubtedly why religious pages are the most popular on Facebook, routinely outranking pop music and movie stars.[3]

FACEBOOK GROUPS

In some cases, congregations and other organizations use a Facebook group instead of, or in addition to, a page. Groups provide more control over who can see content and participate in conversations. They can be "open" so that anyone can join, or "closed," requiring visitors to request permission or be added by the administrator.

In our estimation, it makes sense to create closed groups when the conversation is meant to be more intimate and unguarded. For example, we know of churches that use Facebook to enrich the space between face-to-face covenant groups and spiritual guidance groups. And, certainly, groups for teens and young adults should generally be private.

 When putting church or organizational content on Facebook, put it on your group page first and then share it from there to your personal profile. A link to your group Facebook page will automatically be included in your post.

However, we chafe at the idea of religious groups of a more general nature—Bible study, for instance, or social concerns groups—being closed to "outsiders." Access to such groups can give visitors and inquirers insight into the workings of your community, offer welcome, and form the basis of relationships that may develop further in face-to-face

engagement and worship. We are particularly troubled when we come across church pages—the Yellow Pages listing of the Internet—that are closed to outsiders. Such practices may salve an anxiety about eroding Digital Age privacy, but they send the worst kind of message to those seeking to learn about your church or organization. It just seems, well, unchristian.

Members of the groups, by default, receive notifications by email (which they can turn off, if they wish). The benefit here is that they won't miss the message on your Facebook page, if they don't happen to be on Facebook that day.

Groups are best for internal communication. It is common to use Facebook groups for smaller groupings within the congregation. With features like group chat, for example, or the ability to share documents and post events and pictures, they are equally useful for youth groups or church committees.

Good Shepherd Lutheran Church in Fayetteville, Arkansas, for example, has a vibrant Facebook group for the congregation. Pastor Clint Schenkloth actively posts, which encourages others to post as well. Sermon teasers, church and local events, sometimes random thoughts, and announcements illuminate the group. Members share pictures, blog posts, sermons. Frequent likes and comments show a high degree of engagement and interaction.

BADGES

It used to be that having a website gave you all the credibility you needed online. Today, that credibility comes from having a Facebook presence—and, to a lesser extent, other social media involvement. Not having a Facebook

presence is like not having a website or being listed in the phone book. So, it's important to show your Facebook presence on your website, allowing people to connect with you through the webpage. Facebook provides snippets of code that you can insert into your webpage to link to your Facebook page. As the website for Project F-M (which we discuss in Chapter 4) illustrates, a badge will allow you to make linkages between platforms easily.

As we noted at the beginning of the chapter, Facebook is by far the most accessible, easiest to use social network with the furthest demographic reach. You'll definitely want to start your digital ministry there. But if you've already been on Facebook for a while, you can still grow your digital ministry skills. Before moving on to Twitter, assess where you are in Facebook digital ministry expertise:

Novice

- Create a Facebook profile that includes

  - A casual picture of yourself; if you're clergy, this can be in a collar, but make sure it's a relaxed, rather than formal photo that will make you more relatable
  - Some basic information about you, your background, and your interests
  - Some photos that will give people a sense of your everyday life

- Link to personal and church platforms
- "Like" other people's posts, ten times a week
- Notice people's birthdays and celebrate a bit with them by posting a birthday greeting on their page
- Make friend requests to people already in your personal and professional networks
- Let your church or organization know you're active on Facebook in a newsletter, email list, or other regular communication (like a sermon)

Oblate

- Post at least three times a week
- Comment on others' posts at least once a day
- Add more information to your profile like music preferences or favorite quotes
- Actively share links to online news and magazine articles that you think will be of interest to people in your network
- Practice offering a "Quote of the Week" or an inspirational photo
- Create a group or page for your organization and invite friends to join
- Add photos of your community in action (and reflection) to the group or page

Superior

- Post at least twice a day, once in the morning and once in the afternoon

- Use weekend slow-read time for in-depth articles and blog links
- Invite engagement by asking questions and facilitating conversation
- Post a mix of content: pictures, video, text, check-ins
- Tag people in your posts
- Connect your Facebook page(s) to other social media platforms, like Twitter, Foursquare, and your blog

3.2 TWITTER

Number of Users	175 million registered users
Typical User	African-American and Latino males between age 24 and 36 See Chapter 1 for more details
Key Features	• Personal profile • Tweets, retweets, mentions, direct messages, hashtags
Benefits of Participation	• Connect with people beyond your existing networks • Drive interest in your blog, Facebook page, or website • Establish thought leadership
Limitations	• 140-character format is difficult for some to master • Popularity among marketers and advertisers
Cost	• Free • Sponsored tweets and profiles available
Parallel Platforms	• Posterous • FriendFeed (These have very small communities.)

THE BASICS

Twitter is a micro-blogging platform, with every post limited to 140 characters, including spaces between words. Like blog posts, tweets tell a story in real time through short bursts of commentary and information. Likewise, the aggregation of tweets over time tells a more extended story. Indeed, the personal, institutional, and social narrative that is unfolding on Twitter is seen as so significant that the Smithsonian Institution has been collecting everything ever tweeted for future study by scholars and other cultural commentators. Given the diverse participation by people of faith on Twitter, scholars now have an enormous body of data on current religious beliefs, spiritual practices, and other elements in global religious life.

Twitter is an open platform—that is, anyone can see your tweets, whether or not they follow you—that allows you to:

- Comment on news and events
- Participate in open conversations
- Create new contacts
- Develop professional connections
- Participate in a broader conversation

- Invite people to your website by linking to the webpage and other online profiles
- Coordinate groups for social action
- Connect with people on the go, since Twitter is largely a mobile platform

Twitter doesn't reach as many people as Facebook, but it reaches people in a very different way, a more open way that is very good for engaging influential thinkers within and beyond the larger church, who tend to be very active on Twitter. Whereas Facebook leverages your existing real-life social network, Twitter connects you to people beyond your existing relationships. You can find people with similar interests and join in geographically—often globally— distributed public conversations. It's relatively easy to find people with common interests by simply typing any word or phrase into the Twitter search bar.

For the most part, then, you can follow anyone on Twitter. While some people do "lock" their Twitter profiles so that you have to request permission to follow, as with Facebook friends, this practice is not common on Twitter. That means that you're able to follow pretty much any church, religious organization, ministry colleague, religious thinker, writer, and so on whose minute-by-minute, day-by-day thinking interests you. And, it's very likely that many of these people will follow you back, opening the door to tweeted dialogue. It's for this reason that Pastor David Hansen calls Twitter his "online ministerium."

If you are worried about spam, you may want to use a Twitter validation service, like TruTwit, that filters out spam. You can post pictures and video using services like TwitPic and yFrog, but Twitter is mainly text and link driven. It is good for pointing to websites, blog posts with links that connect people to your blog or website, links to news, and other items of interest.

YOUR TWITTER PROFILE

A Twitter profile is significantly less comprehensive than your Facebook profile. It includes a photo, a 160-character self-description, your location, and a link to a website if you have one. If you don't have a personal or organizational website, you can use your Facebook address, which appears in the address bar every time you visit your profile page, as your web address.

This will give people access only to what you have set as "public" in your privacy settings.

In Twitter, people get to know you much less from the way you present yourself on your profile than from how you hold yourself in conversation. Wit and succinct substance are virtues on Twitter, so you want to take care even with your self-description. Make sure to spend some time looking at other people's profiles to get a sense of the cultural norms in your neck of the Twitter neighborhood.

Once you've joined Twitter, you create and update your profile from the settings tab in the pull-down menu below your user name on the top right of the Twitter screen:

Once you're in "settings," you'll want to focus on filling out your profile:

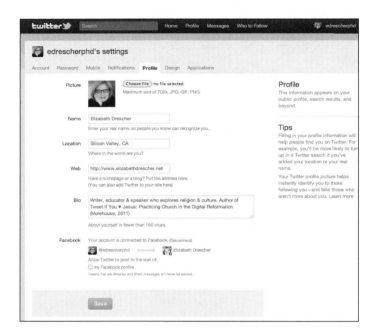

Note that the default profile image for Twitter is an egg icon—commonly referred to as the "Egghead" icon among people active on Twitter. Nothing says, "I'd really rather not get to know anyone" quite like the Egghead. Some people (Elizabeth among them) will often not bother to follow or follow-back someone who didn't take the time to post a photo. So, make sure to include an actual photo of yourself, or at least a cartoonized version that allows people to get a quick sense of who you are when they see your profile.

From the profile tab in settings, you can move to the design tab to select one of nineteen background designs or to upload your own artwork to further enhance the "you-ness" of your Twitter profile. That's pretty much all it takes to get started.

Below are some of the basics of entering the Twitter conversation, but it's probably a good idea to take some time listening to the conversation before you jump in. As you wade in, it's a good practice to begin with retweets of other people's tweets. This both gives you meaningful content to share and shows that you're paying attention to others' ideas.

TWTSPK

Twtspk and Txtspk—abbreviations for Twitterspeak and Textspeak—is the abbreviated lexicon drawn from cell phone texting that helps tweeters to keep tweets short. For the most part, this involves dropping vowels and using the first letters of common phrases, as in the well-known LOL, "laughing out loud." A huge variety of websites offer Twtspk dictionaries—just Google "Twitter abbreviations."

But it's important not to go overboard. Everyone doesn't use the same abbreviations, and abbreviations for complex thoughts can be particularly confusing. Moreover, the idea of Twitter is to keep it short so conversation can move along among groups of followers. Even if you were able to get the Lord's Prayer down to 140 characters, no one would really want to decode and read it.

HASHTAGS

Hashtags are words or short phases (without spaces between words) that begin with the # symbol. These are ways of organizing conversations. Sometimes they are used for fun, but even a joke can build connections and extend communities. For example, two Roman Catholic tweeters started

PRAYING THE MANHUNT ON TWITTER

 Many of the community leaders in our town—from our library, Boys and Girls Clubs, YMCA, to community organizers, activists, and neighbors—are active on Twitter. I have been able to interact with them, share information, become more aware of their work, and make them more aware of ours.

This all came to have much more than social meaning in the late summer of 2011, when a police officer was shot while responding to a robbery at a local jewelry store.

Twitter immediately lit up about the incident, with tweets from news outlets, community leaders, and residents. Most people used the hashtag #woburn—the general hashtag we use for community information—to tag their posts. For the rest of the day, Woburn was trending on Twitter. So, I jumped in and started retweeting posts.

One suspect had been apprehended. Three other suspects were on the loose, considered armed and dangerous. It was a manhunt. Local and state police, SWAT teams, helicopters

Continued

what turned into a days-long series of tweets about the quirks of the Roman Catholic Church when they jokingly used the hashtag #CatholicRulesFor

PRAYING THE MANHUNT ON TWITTER *Continued*

were all on scene. There were road blocks. Door-to-door searches. Schools and the YMCA were in lock down. Residents were urged to stay inside with their doors locked.

It was chilling. One person tweeted, "Police searching the woods near my house in west #Woburn. I can see them out the window. This is very scary."

I was retweeting news and information as quickly as it came in.

Then I realized that my role, not only as a resident of Woburn, but as a minster in this community, was to try to offer some measure of solace, support, and to point to God's presence in a horrific and confusing situation. So, I began to tweet prayers:

> We pray for the safety of #Woburn residents and the police. Lord have mercy.

> We pray that his manhunt comes to a just and peaceful conclusion. Lord have mercy. #Woburn

> We pray for those who weep and watch and work this night. Lord have mercy. #Woburn

Continued

Twitter. Within minutes, other Roman Catholic tweeters had joined in the fun, and tweeters from other denominations started sharing #Anglican RulesForTwitter, #LutheranRulesFor Twitter, #UCCRulesForTwitter, and so on. The joke circled the globe, morphing from English to Spanish to Latin, French, and Italian.

Within a few days, Jesuit writer James Martin, SJ, was blogging about the phenomenon and Elizabeth was writing about it in the *San Francisco Chronicle*. The originators of the hashtag, @sullijo (Jonathan Sullivan) and @vitacatholic, a DC blogger named Rae, called on tweeps (or people active on Twitter) to design a #CatholicRulesForTwitter logo that could be used on swag like mugs and mouse pads, the sale of which benefits the nonprofit Catholic Relief.

Most of the time, however, hashtags organize somewhat more pedestrian—though no less engaging—conversations. For instance, on Tuesday evenings at 9:00 p.m. Eastern there is a social media and church tweetchat that is organized with the hashtag #chsocm, short for Church and Social Media. Created by writer Meridith Gould, the #chsocm hashtag organizes a meeting place for community and conversation between chats throughout the week. Existing communities, like Keith's hometown of Woburn, will designate a commonly agreed upon hashtag, here #Woburn, for community-related tweets.

Hashtags are also used for specific events. Church conferences often designate a hashtag for that event. For example, people who wanted to follow the Episcopal Church's last General Convention in 2009 could hunt for tweets with the hashtag #ecgc (count on something similar at the next gathering in 2012).

When deciding on what hashtag to use for your event or topic, search Twitter first to see if anyone else is using it. Choosing a specific hashtag helps filter out the noise.

MENTIONS/SHOUT-OUTS

Anytime someone includes your Twitter handle in a tweet, it shows up in the "@ Connect" tab on your Twitter home page and, if you have elected in your settings to do so, you will receive an email notification. Mentions are a standard part of Twitter conversations, where all responses begin with the Twitter name being responded to. If you want to bring someone else into the conversation, add their Twitter handle. This is also a good way to acknowledge someone as meaningful in your social media universe. Such acknowledgements are commonly referred to as "shout-outs," and they are valuable social capital on Twitter.

Many tweeps observe #FF or Follow Friday, when they recommend some of the people they follow on Twitter to others. This is an effective way to do a collective "shout-out," introducing those who influence you to others in your Twitter network.

PRAYING THE MANHUNT ON TWITTER *Continued*

I know these prayers connected because they were retweeted by members of the Woburn community—ordinary residents and leaders alike. Kathi Johnson, a tweeter from Texas, even appropriated one of the prayers for the central Texas fires.

> "We pray for those who weep and watch and work this night. Lord have mercy. #Woburn #centraltxfires"

She said later, "It struck me how tenuous both situations are and the prayer seemed right for this, too."

At an earlier community event I joked about being a "Twitter chaplain," but on that day it was no joke. And I was pastor to a community of people in Woburn and beyond that were trying to make sense of the violence and tragedy that had just happened.

RETWEETS [RT]

Retweeting is a way of sharing a tweet that someone else has written. You might share it because it's useful, fun, or because you want to give someone a shout-out. By default, the person retweeted receives an email notification, so they will know you've noticed their tweet and shared it with your network. You can retweet verbatim by clicking the "retweet" option below each tweet. The retweet [RT] will show up in your Twitter feed with the handle of the original tweeter.

You can also "retweet with comment" and add your own little editorial by copying the original tweet (with the tweeter's handle, of course), pasting it into your status box, and adding your comment at the beginning or end. Do this when possible because it makes clear to your followers that you're really attending to what they tweet rather than just randomly retweeting (which some social media "experts" advise).

Retweets are gold in Twitter because they multiply your social capital by extending the content you create and share to all of your followers and their followers and so on, and so on, exponentially. The key, then, is to create content that can easily be retweeted because it's pithy, original, engaging, and readily sharable and to retweet generously across your network.

DIRECT MESSAGES [DM]

These are private messages sent back and forth directly between two Twitter users. It's like email, but limited, like everything on Twitter, to 140 characters.

LISTS

Even though tweets are only 140 characters, if you follow enough people, it can be hard to keep up. One way to organize tweets from various followers is to create lists for different groupings of tweeps. You might have a list for parishioners, community leaders, other ministers, or people who share your interests.

Lists are also curated by other Twitter users, allowing you to enjoy the benefit of others' organizing and collaborative efforts. The "Techreligerati" list, for instance, is a public list curated by Frank Santoni (@fsantoni) through his Techreligious project (@techreligious on Twitter, with links to the techreligious. com website). Santoni, a Roman Catholic technophile and general do-gooder with a strong ecumenical streak, draws together "thought leaders" in religion and technology through the Twitter list, and offers more in-depth commentary on the Techreligious site.

FEEDING TWITTER FROM FACEBOOK

If you'd like to have a presence on Twitter, but don't have time to manage it, you can send content from your Facebook group page to a Twitter account. First, create a Twitter account and then go to http://www.facebook.com/twitter/. There you can link your Facebook page with the Twitter account. Once linked, everything posted on your Facebook page will be automatically sent to your Twitter feed. Messages longer than 140 characters will be assigned a link to the Facebook page.

You can also go the opposite direction, feeding from Twitter to your personal or group Facebook page. To do this, go back to your Twitter profile page, and click in the check box at the bottom of the page to permit Twitter access to your Facebook account.

WIDGETS FOR YOUR WEBSITE

Compared to other platforms like Facebook and YouTube, Twitter is used by a much smaller community, but hardly one leaders in ministry can ignore. You can make your Twitter feed accessible to those people who aren't on Twitter by putting a Twitter widget on your website. Go to *http://twitter.*

SOCIAL MEDIA DASHBOARDS

 A number of desktop, smartphone, and tablet computer applications—apps—are available to help you manage your participation on Twitter, and coordinate it with Facebook, Foursquare, LinkedIn, and other social networking platforms. Free versions of these apps are available, but they also have paid upgrades.

The most popular of these "dashboards" is TweetDeck, which is owned by Twitter. Also used extensively is HootSuite. These tools allow you to schedule tweets and posts to your various social media sites in advance. So, for instance, you can set up inspirational quotes to roll out through the week, saving you the worry of keeping up on that variety of social media participation.

The downside, however, is that many in the social networking community are uncomfortable with the feel of such pre-set tweets and quotes, which can seem more like broadcast marketing than social engagement. They may save you time, but limit relationship-building.

com/widgets to create and customize your own widget. Based on your selections, Twitter will provide you a snippet of code to embed on your website. This gives your site an instant news stream and publicizes your Twitter feed.

Almost everyone we know in ministry who uses Twitter has taken a while to warm to the genre. In part, this is because Twitter is used extensively for advertising and for the often narcissistic ramblings of celebrities. It gets noisy quickly. And, most of us in ministry are, well, a bit committed to the Word in its more verbose forms. As Elizabeth has said of her self-described "lazy blogger" practice, "Three or four paragraphs? I'm just getting warmed up by then!"

But when you take care in selecting a community of tweeters to follow, and develop lists that help you to organize various conversations, participating on Twitter can be a richly rewarding experiencing, connecting you to a worldwide community of believers and seekers who are anxious to be in conversation about many issues facing the church. As we saw in Chapter 1, Twitter is particularly popular among African Americans and Latina/o Americans, demographics that are sorely underrepresented in most mainline churches. That fact alone is reason enough to join in the conversation.

As you get started, or as you plan to raise the bar on your Twitter participation, take some time to reflect on your current level of expertise:

Novice

- Include a picture of yourself smiling
- Develop a succinct, perhaps witty, description
- Link your profile to personal or church website
- Retweet at least once a day
- Try a #FF list

Oblate

- Tweet three to five times a day
- Share content from your blog and Facebook
- Using mentions, engage others in conversation (you don't have to know them)
- Use an aggregator such as bit.ly, dig.com, or ow.ly to track tweet themes
  of interest to you and your community
- Use hashtags both for humor and to highlight your community and its interests

Superior

- Tweet several times daily
- Use an application such as HootSuite or TweetDeck to schedule tweets through the day or week and manage messages, mentions, retweets, and trends
- Integrate other applications, such as Foursquare and Facebook, with your Twitter feed
- Participate in tweetchats and other live tweet events
- Live-tweet an event
- Attend a local tweetup

3.3 LINKEDIN

Number of Users	• 120 million members • Largest professional social network
Typical User	• 59% male • 35% between 25 and 34 • 35% between 36 and 50 • Nearly 1 million are teachers • 50% outside of the United States
Key Features	• Personal profile • Personal and institutional pages • Groups • Posting of status updates, photos, links to other content, videos, chat
Benefits of Participation	Reach professionals who don't participate in other social networks
Limitations	Annoying advertising
Cost	Free, but premium content available for an annual fee
Parallel Platforms	• Biznik—For entrepreneurs • Focus—For IT professionals • Young Entrepreneur (All of these have very small, specialized communities and none is particularly appropriate for religious or spiritual engagement.)

THE BASICS

LinkedIn is the last of the major social media platforms that should be a part of your digital ministry strategy. LinkedIn is a good option for reaching professionals in your congregation, who may be on LinkedIn (or are more active on LinkedIn), but not other networking sites. In some cases, people are prohibited by their employers from social spaces like Facebook and blogs, but are permitted to be on LinkedIn for professional and business purposes. Generally, because fewer people are on LinkedIn, and because (as we'll discuss below) you can feed updates from Twitter, the bulk of the time you spend on the site will involve setting up your profile. After that, it's probably sufficient to check in on a monthly basis.

Some churches and church organizations have set up groups for church professionals or alumni to help members network with one another or,

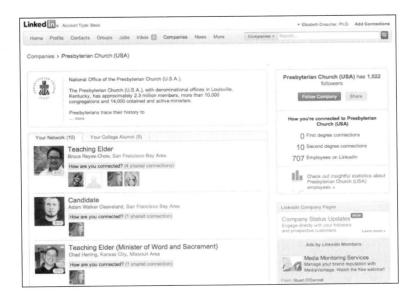

in some cases, the wider community. Most national denominations have LinkedIn profiles and groups. Exploring such groups will provide another option for connecting with colleagues and sharing some of your community's story.

This kind of business and professional social network is fertile ground to tell a story about vocation—setting ministry in the context of daily life along with other professions. Posts, discussions, and messages can help support people seeking to live faithfully in the midst of their work day. This is not always an area of people's lives that the church does a good job understanding and supporting. Our presence on LinkedIn or similar business networks can help.

LinkedIn is valuable for:

- Connecting with people who aren't on other sites
- Connecting with professionals in your congregation and connecting them to one another
- Establishing credibility in your field and among other professionals
- Establishing a presence on a highly popular site for business professionals

SETTING UP YOUR LINKEDIN PROFILE

The LinkedIn profile is essentially an online resume. You don't need to complete it in extensive detail, but enough so that people know your basic work and educational background. Part of the appeal of LinkedIn is that it helps people establish credibility and authority in a particular field by displaying their education and experience as well as by participating in discussions within their field. That is the lifeblood of LinkedIn, so you really do want to make sufficient information available to get you into the conversation. You can also post links and information to your profile and, if you are on Twitter, you can link accounts so that your tweets will appear on your profile.

LinkedIn is all about making connections, so it should come as no surprise that when you sign up the first thing you'll see are prompts to connect to friends or colleagues who may already be members by sharing access to your email address book. You can skip this step, which will usually result in seeing a prompt to purchase premium membership. Premium memberships allow you access to emailing features and allow you to do more sophisticated searches for contacts. These are typically of value to people in sales, marketing, or employment recruiting.

There's not usually much value to individual members or organizations like churches. So, you can skip this step as well, and head on to create your profile.

Setting up a profile for you or your organization is perhaps more straightforward on LinkedIn than on any of the other social networks because the formatting is very standardized. Aside from your personal photo—which

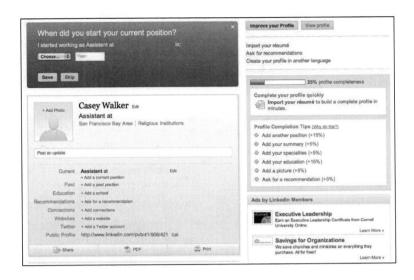

you want to make sure to include so you don't appear anonymous—all the information you share is in standard categories that you update on the profile page.

To get there, click on the profile tab in the pulldown menu at the top of the LinkedIn home screen, and select "Edit Profile" from the menu.

Basic profile information includes current and past positions, education, and your organizational or personal website address. You can share employment and educational information as you like, but it can be interesting for people to see the breadth and depth of work and educational experience people bring into ministry, so don't be too shy about sharing your degree in molecular gastronomy or the five years you worked on a crab trawler.

The profile edit form also asks you to add connections—your social network on LinkedIn, like friends on Facebook and followers on Twitter. If you're not comfortable sharing your email password to look through your address book, you can do a people search on the top of the page for the names of people you might like to add. Both Keith and Elizabeth are on LinkedIn, and we would be happy to connect with you to get you going. But it's best, of course, to connect to people who are likely to have a more direct link to you and your community. So, as with Facebook and Twitter, it's good to let people in your networks know you've joined LinkedIn. At the bottom of the edit profile page, you'll see a web address for your public profile—the one that can be seen by people who are not yet connections. Copy and paste this into a status update for Facebook or a tweet announcing you're now a LinkedIn member and would be happy to connect with members of your networks.

CONNECTIONS

Connections work somewhat like friend requests on Facebook. On LinkedIn, everyone you ask to be a connection must approve your request. This allows you to send private emails to the connection. However, somewhat as on Twitter, everyone on LinkedIn can see your public profile.

When you send a connection invitation, you will be prompted to identify your connection to the person you're inviting, and you'll have the opportunity to leave a short note. LinkedIn gives you a generic message, but you have the opportunity to customize, making your message to a potential contact more personal.

RECOMMENDATIONS

The profile edit screen also asks you to request recommendations from colleagues. These are more or less generic recommendations for the purpose of job-seeking or sales. In most cases, they don't have a purpose in ministry. That said, if you are creating a group page for your church or organization, it may not be inappropriate to ask members of your community to offer personal recommendations that share something of a personal perspective on your community.

As noted above, you also have the opportunity to connect your LinkedIn account to Twitter. This is a good idea because you're likely to be less active on LinkedIn than on other networks. Although LinkedIn has recently tried to enhance the user experience on the site by adding a news feed with articles related to what their algorithms discern as your areas of interest, it's nonetheless the case that most people—perhaps especially those in religious organizations and related non-profits—tend to visit the site only as professional need dictates. Having a feed from Twitter will keep your LinkedIn profile active in what may turn out to be the long lag between visits. Elizabeth, for instance, only visits LinkedIn when she receives an email letting her know that someone has sent her a message or asked her to confirm them as a connection, but her Twitter feed keeps her present there in between formal visits.

GROUPS

You might consider creating a LinkedIn group for your congregation, organization, or group. Like a Facebook group, a LinkedIn group can be open, so that anyone can join, or a closed group that requires permission from an administrator to join. At the very least, a group can make members who are already on LinkedIn aware of one another's presence there. In the work of social media in ministry, the more connections we can build, the better. There, people can learn about the work and skills of their fellow members. In some cases, it may even help in their career path.

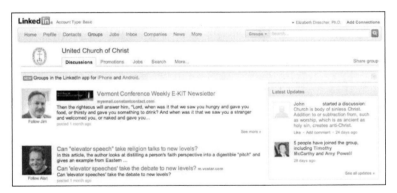

For group content, called "discussions," you can configure your group page to grab content from any blog using the RSS feed web address. This automatically shares blog posts and YouTube playlists. You can also post links to articles you think would be edifying to the group. Members of the group can comment and discuss it.

As we've noted, most people in ministry use LinkedIn in fairly limited ways, planting a flag for the church or organization without really settling in. By and large, this is a reasonable approach unless your congregation is made up of lots of business professionals or you hope to connect with such people. In that case, it's important to consider the steps you'll need to take to move from novice to superior level:

Novice

- Create a full profile with your educational and work history and a professional picture
- Find members of your congregation and invite them to be connections
- Announce your participation on LinkedIn in your newsletter, on your blog, on Facebook, and on Twitter

Oblate

- Create a group for your church, organization, or ministry
- Invite people to join the group by including the link on Facebook, Twitter, congregational email, or newsletter
- Set up any RSS (Real Simple Syndication) feeds you may have to appear in group discussions (See Glossary for details on an RSS feed, which allows visitors to subscribe and receive updates when new posts are added.)

Superior

- Post discussion topics in your group; encourage people to respond
- Post job openings in your church
- Get recommendations from friends, which will appear on your profile

3.4 BLOGS

Number of Users	Over 150,000,000 blogs
Typical User[4]	• About 50% female, 50% male • 53% between age 21 and 35 • 70% outside of the U.S.
Key Features	• Posts • Photos • Comments • Categorize, tag, and search content • Links to Twitter and Facebook
Benefits of Participation	• More space to share your story • Genre is more familiar to ministry types
Limitations	• Too much space to share your story • Takes more time to create content and maintain blog site
Cost	Free, paid upgrades available
Popular Blogging Platforms	*Wordpress.com, Blogger.com, Typepad.com, Posterous.com, Tumblr.com*

THE BASICS

Once you have a presence on the major social networking sites, it's important to begin generating original content to share with your digital community. The whole idea of sharing your story is to bring your unique perspective on the world, the church, and ministry to a wider community and engage in conversation. While your profiles will show that, and the links you share will highlight your interests, you also want to illustrate how you practice ministry, how you bring your faith and your training together in service of others. Creating your own content is a vital part of this aspect of digital ministry, and blogging is typically a good first step. Since most ministry training revolves

SHOULD YOU BLOG YOUR SERMONS?

As Keith has noted, ministry leaders often start blogging by way of sharing sermons. However, it's important to note that the sermon and the blog are two very different genres. The sermon generally assumes an existing relationship in a community. It can take a certain shared history

Continued

**SHOULD YOU BLOG
YOUR SERMONS?** *Continued*

for granted. And, it relies extensively on nonverbal elements like tone, inflection, and gesture that often do not translate smoothly into written form.

So, should you forget about a sermon blog? Not necessarily. Many churches include a sermon blog on their website so that people who were unable to attend services can at least read the sermon and those who were present have the opportunity for further reflection. But this is a fairly specialized, and unusual, use of the blog genre, which tends to be much shorter and more narrowly focused than the average sermon.

If you do intend to blog your sermon for a more general readership outside your community, it's best to edit it down to three or four paragraphs—the real money part of your sermon—and to highlight the points you think are most important. Adding a photo to illustrate your points will help to adapt your sermon to the blog genre.

around communicating through the written word, blogs tend to be the most familiar form of storytelling for ministry leaders. The longer written content of blogging is the closest (though not the same) social media genre to sermons and newsletter articles. Indeed, many leaders in ministry start blogging long before they enter other social networking communities.

Frequently, churches and individual ministers use blogs to post sermons, to share ideas about or beyond church, and as an online journal or travelogue. Here, stories unfold in each post but also across posts, creating a nuanced, detailed, theologically reasoned arc.

Some commentators have indicated that blogging is on its way out.[5] Blogging ranks among the least popular forms of social media engagement. However, while that might be true, there are still millions of people blogging and reading blogs that they share across their networks. Furthermore, for those who blog well, it remains a highly influential genre.

Blogs are also useful places to experiment, reflect, work out ideas, and solicit feedback, particularly from those beyond your particular ministry setting.

Blogs are good for:

- Developing and sharing your ideas
- Becoming identified as a "thought leader" in the church on your area of interest
- Becoming a better writer and showcasing your writing

- Starting or influencing conversations in your areas of interest
- Serving as a personal webpage
- Accumulating content over time
- Telling a more detailed personal and ministry story
- Offering mission interpretation and theological reflection
- Making content like sermons, newsletters, and articles easily sharable and searchable
- Documenting an individual's or community's journey

Blogs are a powerful way to share ideas and establish yourself as a "thought leader"—someone with particular influence in your area of interest—by creating an online portfolio of your ideas and writing, which are archived, categorized, and searchable. The advantage of having a blog, rather than just posting on Facebook in the longer-form "notes" feature (see below), is that the blog will aggregate and organize your portfolio. In social networks, content is fleeting, with much of what is shared having the useful life of a day. Blogs participate in this rapid-change environment, but they are also built for the long haul.

POSTING PRACTICE

Posts are the heart of your blog. You'll no doubt have your own style, but conventional wisdom says that individual posts should be limited to about five hundred words. Above five hundred words, consider breaking it into multiple posts. Always include at least one picture in your post because a thumbnail appears when you share on social networks, creating more visual interest so that people will be more likely to click on it. Break up the text through subheadings, and keep paragraphs to two to four short sentences. Take advantage of hyperlinks—digital connections (links) to other websites, documents, photos, or videos. Rather than

BLOGGING GOOD ENOUGH TO EAT!

You might also begin blogging on a different passion. David Crowley, president of Social Capital, Inc. (profiled in Chapter 4), began a cooking blog, Cookingchat, as a way to become proficient in blogging before he used it for work.

Elaine Murray Dreeben takes it a bit further. A Presbyterian seminarian from Louisville, Kentucky, Dreeben blogs as The Reverend Chef, linking

Continued

BLOGGING GOOD ENOUGH TO EAT! *Continued*

her passion for food and faith (and wine) in a delightfully playful and thought-provoking blog:

Dreeben connects to her blog from her Twitter feed:

And from a Facebook Page:

explaining, link to sources or other content that illustrates what you're discussing. This will keep your text focused and lean.

It's a good idea to read your blog posts three times before you finalize them. First I look at the design on the site. Is this a place someone would want to spend the next few minutes? Is it visually welcoming? If the design is clunky and not done with care, visitors to your blog will expect that the text will be the same.

Second, glance at the title and subheadings to get a sense of the content and trajectory of the post. Does this go somewhere? Do the subtitles themselves express the theme or tone of the post? They don't have to be like the headings of ancient theological tomes (*Paragraph One, In Which I Explain the Purpose of Paragraph One*). But they do need to generate interest, invite engagement, and express something of who you are and what you're hoping to share.

Third, if the blog post passes those two tests, actually read the text from beginning to end. Reading it aloud doesn't hurt. While most of your visitors won't do this, it does give you a sense of the pace and the tone that will find its way into people's imaginations as they read.

Have a regular schedule for posting. Choose a pattern that you can commit to. It may only be twice a month. In starting out, consistency and quality are more important than volume. Likewise, be consistent in your content. Focus on a few key areas, so those readers know what to expect. It's okay to throw in an off-topic post every now and then, but don't make it a habit.

Pastor Chris Duckworth of Grace Lutheran Church in St. Paul, Minnesota, has been blogging at *The Lutheran Zephyr* since 2004 and says, "You've got to be really clear about what the heck you're doing or else you're going to be rambling. And once you set it up, as with anything, you've got to do it. You can't set up a blog and then let your last blog post be nine months ago."

Duckworth also recommends that bloggers periodically reevaluate the focus and purpose of their blogs:

TAGS AND TAGGING

 Like "platform," "tag" is a word that has multiple uses in social media.

Tags for blogs indicate subject matter of your content. For your readers, they help sort at the more granular level.

Tags are also built into the page information read by search engines. Include your name, general keywords that describe your blog, and terms specific to your blog post.

The major blog hosting sites include a section to enter tags in the control panel.

See section 3.1 for a discussion of tagging on Facebook.

> It's like when you're in high school or college and you've been dating someone or you're more like friends or you're kind of dating and you need to have the Define the Relationship conversation. We call those DTRs. I feel like every now and then I need to have a DTR with my blog. What am I doing with this? Why am I doing this?

Finally, anytime you publish anything online, you are writing for multiple audiences. Write for your primary audience, whether that's colleagues, members, the community, or friends—but be aware of your secondary audiences. Assume that everyone in your social network will see it. So, for example, even if you're primarily writing for ministry colleagues, you can be sure that plenty of people outside of that circle will have access to your thoughts. Don't say anything in public, even if you mean to be talking only with a specific group of friends, if you wouldn't want *everyone* known and unknown to you to hear.

BLOG CATEGORIES AND TAGS

Categories and tags help organize your posts. A blog should have a small number of main categories. For example, Keith's blog posts are organized under three main categories: Social Media, Spirituality, and Church. These are the main subjects of your blog. Each category can have a larger number of sub-categories. You can have an unlimited number of tags in each post.

Like categories and sub-categories, tags make your content sortable. If someone clicks on a tag, they'll see all the other posts with the same tag. Tags are also important for helping you get discovered on search engines. Tags appear in the webpage information, which search engines read and catalog. Always include your name, location, and church, along with some keywords from the subject matter.

ABOUT PAGE

A good "about" page—the page on your blog that introduces you to visitors—is crucial to blogging success. Some say it is the most important page on your blog, and it consistently ranks as one of the most visited pages. Once people engage your ideas—or often before they do—they want

to know a little bit about who you are. So, it's important to prominently link to the about page. Be sure to include a picture, information about you and your blog, and a brief description of your areas of interest. For instance, the "About Me" page for Presbyterian minister and popular blogger Adam Copeland's "A Wee Blether" blog includes a bit of background on his current ministry setting, a note on the topics that tend to appear in his blog, and some humanizing, personal information on his "affection for sharp cheddar, local beers, and contemporary fiction" and his "brilliant and beautiful" wife, Megan. He also includes a "quick bio" and a Facebook widget on his about page.

SHORT FORM BLOGGING

As Keith has mentioned—and as Elizabeth has highlighted—the blog genre is characterized by relatively brief discussion. Popular blogs by, for example, progressive Evangelical Rachel Held Evans (rachelheldevans.com) or speculative religionista Nathan Schneider (theRowBoat.com) get down and pithy in just a few short paragraphs. But even shorter forms of blogging have grown in popularity. The blog hosting site Tumblr, in particular, has become a popular platform for what we might call "mini-blogs" that offer a combination of multimedia content: pictures, short text, video, quotes. Many people keep one of each kind of blog—long form blog for more finished content, short form blog for sharing side interests or developing ideas.

Sister Heather Rollins, the Undercover Nun, uses Tumblr as her main blog. She says, "For a non-geek who was just starting out with a blog, I would recommend Tumblr with no hesitation. It has much better social features, so it's a lot easier to build up a following and engage with people quickly, compared to the more traditional blogging platforms."

Those social features led to deeper connections. "I connected, particularly from Tumblr, with some people who had asked for counsel, and we ended up in a relationship that was almost like spiritual direction. I was just amazed when this started to happen."

PUBLICIZING YOUR POSTS

There are millions upon millions of blogs floating across cyberspace. Mostly, no one ever reads them. This is because the majority of bloggers don't let

AT TABLE
St. Lydia's Dinner Church

 Inspired by the practice of agape meals of the early church, St. Lydia's Dinner Church in New York City gathers for worship around the dinner table. Led by pastoral minister Emily Scott and community coordinator Rachel Pollak, they gather before worship to prepare the evening's meal, and then share the sermon, prayers, and communion as part of the meal. The life of St. Lydia's is marked by food, community, and poetry.

Emily observes, "We're using social media and technology to advance what we're doing as a community, and yet a lot of what we do on Sunday nights is really countercultural in terms of its engagement with technology. In some ways we're engaging with a high-tech, modern world, and in other ways when you walk into our space, it's completely pre-technological."

One of the ways they strike a balance between pre-tech and high-tech is through their blog, At Table. The design of the blog itself incorporates a mix of old and new, with scanned fabrics as

Continued

others know they've shared new content. Some of them are happy with that. Their blogging is more of a digital diary that will flicker on in obscurity until anthropologists in some far off future come upon it quite by accident. In the context of digital ministry, however, you want to share your story so that you can develop and extend relationships. You want to create opportunities for conversation and connection. And, to do that, you will need to get the word out that you'd love to chat with all those who have eyes to see and ears to hear.

Once you have written your post, then, share a link to it on Facebook and Twitter. On Facebook, share a link to the post (not the home page but the post itself) and provide a small quote or short explanation of what it's about. If you mention someone, tag that person.

On Twitter, share the link with a very brief explanation, including the Twitter handle of anyone you mention in the post or of anyone you think might have a particular interest. If it applies, include a hashtag. Keith might add #Woburn for his town, #elca for his national denomination, #chsocm for the church and social media tweetchat community. Elizabeth uses #TEC for "The Episcopal Church," often along with #Anglican, so her tweets are signaled to a wider, global community. (Review hashtags and mentions in section 3.2 on Twitter.)

You can also engage people more directly as you prepare your blog in ways that both improve content quality and enhance its distribution across social networks. For example, you might occasionally share a draft with other bloggers and get feedback. When they become invested in the post, they will be more likely to share with their networks, which may be well developed. They may even blog a response and keep the conversation going. If there are people you want to be sure will see the post, send them the link specifically via email, on Facebook through a private message (see section 3.2), or via Twitter.

You can also mention people you're featuring or whose ideas you're mulling as you're writing the blog on Facebook or Twitter. For example, Elizabeth might post on Facebook or Twitter, "Thinking about @ prkanderson as 'Twitter Chaplain' for next blog post." Such advance comments are likely to generate conversation or at least cue interest in the forthcoming post.

BLOG COMMENTS

A blog post may represent your freshest thinking on a topic, but it is only

---

AT TABLE
St. Lydia's Dinner Church *Continued*

table cloths, woodcuts for artwork, and links to social media sites.

Blog posts include Emily's sermons, Rachel's poetry recommendations, contributions by members of the community, and recipes. All of this tells the story of the community they are creating together.

"If you've been to worship, you can use the blog as a resource," Emily says. "If you're not going to worship, you can also enter into it because there are resources for your own spiritual edification."

Lydians see it as a "scrapbook for the community, almost archival, almost a piece of artwork that is being made about the community."

The community brings their care in welcoming newcomers to their blog, as well. "Something I've been pushing for the blog is that every entry has a little blurb across the top in italics that tells you who this person is, whose voice this is in, and why is this going on," Emily explains. "You're always reintroducing the community to the newcomer and assuming you're not just talking to the insiders."

---

the beginning of the conversation. The comments below the post are where the conversation really begins. Responding to comments made on your posts on the blog itself, as well as on Facebook or Twitter, will encourage people to engage with you and your ideas. There is no need to respond to every comment, but reply to some—especially the more thoughtful and substantive comments or those from people who are new to your network. When people take the time to comment, they appreciate being acknowledged. Otherwise, you're just like every other broadcast medium where an anonymous someone blah, blah, blahs what they think without bothering to pay attention to what anyone else thinks. (Elizabeth calls this "blabcasting.")

On hosting services like Wordpress, the comment systems are built in and can be turned on or off. There are typically a range of options for comment moderation from approving all comments automatically, requiring your approval before they are posted on the site, or blocking certain users. Most of the time comments are constructive and can serve to clarify the ideas in your post. It's a good idea to allow for a range of opinions on your blog—that's how conversations happen—but you do have the right to address people who behave inappropriately.

A good approach to problematic commenters is the same sort of "progressive discipline" we discussed with regard to Facebook earlier. Depending on the tenor of the comment, you might begin by emailing the person and explaining your concerns about the comment, indicating that such comments in the future will result in the person being blocked from the blog. If it comes to that, have no compunction about blocking anyone who is unwilling to participate in a rational, respectful way. As with such people in the rest of our lives, it's seldom helpful to engage in open argument. And, in a social media setting, remember that your responses are always public.

Surprising, remarkable relationships can and do develop out of the insights and ideas—your self-presentation as a minister—that you share on a blog. This opportunity to connect and engage, to extend the welcome that is the centerpiece of Christian ministry, is why we feel so strongly about focusing our participation in social media communities on developing the kind of open, inviting content that builds relationships and strengthens the wider community of faith. It's not so much about your message *per se*—it's not so much about *you* at all—but about the ways in which the words and images you share open the hearts and minds of others to deeper and more engaged, consequential faith.

As you reflect on how blogging currently fits into your personal, professional, or institutional digital ministry strategy, consider where you are on the learning curve and what it will take to move to the next level:

Novice

- Create a blog at a hosted service like *wordpress.com, blogger.com, typepad.com*
- Create a good "about" page with a picture of yourself
- Post at least once a month
- Read other blogs and comment on one other blog a week
- Define the three to five topics you will blog about
- Link to your other social media platforms
- Enable people to sign up by email or RSS (most blog services have this built in)

Oblate

- Post four times a month
- Purchase your own domain name from a service like GoDaddy.com or NetworkSolutions.com
- Add a Twitter widget for fresh content

Superior

- Post more than once a week
- Create a self-hosted, customized blog (*Wordpress.org* is the most popular site that allows extensive customization.)
- Invite guest bloggers to post
- Add a Facebook widget to the blog

3.5 YOUTUBE

Views	3 billion videos viewed every day
Key Features	• Video uploading • Channels, playlists • Easy sharing to social networks
Benefits of Participation	Presence on a hugely popular site
Limitations	• Advertising • Moderate video quality
Cost	Free
Parallel Platforms	Vimeo.com

THE BASICS

Online videos are enormously popular. People are engaging video at increasingly higher rates (about 5%) than other social media. Engagement with video increases with each subsequent generation—the younger the person, the more video they see. For Millennials (eighteen- to thirty-three-year-olds), watching videos is the fourth most popular online activity behind email, search, and social networking. And, because images and music speak beyond language barriers, videos have a huge international attraction.

The web is increasingly the place where people go for video, and YouTube is the web's largest video sharing site, where more than twenty-four hours of video are uploaded every minute. It is also the web's third largest search engine. That means that many of the people who are looking for a church or organization like yours will go to YouTube rather than to Google or Yahoo. They want to see you in action, hear your voice, not just read your words.

YouTube is good for:

- Reaching a large segment of people beyond and within Facebook and Twitter
- Reaching younger generations, who watch video at higher rates
- Creating an online video catalog in a high-traffic area
- Organizing videos into theme-related playlists
- Speaking personally and directly
- Being creative and playful in our message
- Creating and sharing a video response to someone else's video
- Hosting videos for free without storing them on your website

Video is often overlooked or dismissed among those in ministry because of a perceived lack of equipment, time, and resources to make something of professional quality. However, part of the charm of YouTube (and what makes videos popular) is the amateur production value. It turns out to be endearing, funny, real, and authentic when someone creates an engaging video on nothing more than a smartphone. Have you seen the one where the three-year-old recites a Billy Collins poem? There's nothing not to like about that, absent Hollywood production values notwithstanding. The charm and quirkiness of these sorts of videos have had a tremendous influence on television and in movies, where directors imitate the amateur, first-person style of YouTube.

All of this is possible, of course, because it is so much easier to shoot and produce video now than it was even a few years ago. Just about any smartphone can record video these days—some even with high definition video cameras and video editing software on board. Most computers now include built-in webcams, and video editing software is often included, and has become much more user friendly.

The Reverend Matthew Moretz, an Episcopal priest and creator of the YouTube series *Father Matthew Presents* (who we profile in Chapter 4), insists, "If you can learn in seminary how to craft a fifteen-minute archaic rhetorical speech, you can learn how to make video—something that's actually contemporary, something that's actually in the *lingua franca* of the world. This is how people are made who they are—by what they see on video on the ever omnipresent screen."

The average person still watches five hours of television a day and Americans spend around $10 billion a year at movie theaters. Video is a primary way we communicate, and yet, it is largely lacking in mainline churches.

"It's the way people tell stories. Other institutions are telling our stories. They're telling my little ones what Christianity is," says Moretz. "By the time they get in confirmation class, they already know what Christianity is because *Family Guy* told them. They know who Jesus is because they saw him on *South Park*. There's got to be more."

Video allows you to tell an expansive, emotive story, combining voice, physical expression, and visual interest. In just a couple minutes, you can convey a host of ideas. It gives people a much better sense of you and allows you to speak to them at work, at home, and wherever they may be on their smartphone. As one parishioner said when Keith's church began its "2-Minute Bible Study" video series (more on this below), "It's like my pastor came over to my house to tell me about the readings for Sunday."

ARE YOU READY FOR YOUR CLOSE-UP?

As we've discussed, the amateur quality of most YouTube videos is a central element of their charm. You don't need to be Sofia Coppola to create engaging video for your community and those who may be drawn to

it. The video Kim Hinrichs posted on her Facebook wall (see section 3.1 above) had some clean, simple editing, but it's hardly as slickly produced as a choir scene from *Sister Act*. Still, the video shows not just a worship leader and choir in ministry, but a congregation at prayer in a church filled with the symbols of faith and hope that have inspired believers through the centuries. At a bit over four minutes, the video is longer than we would typically recommend (more on this shortly). Nonetheless, someone exploring First Plymouth UCC would get a very good sense of how the community functions musically, liturgically, and spiritually that goes far beyond what they might read in a printed brochure.

Videos like this can be made with simple, inexpensive video cameras, flip cameras, and even smartphone cameras. Everyone can get involved. For instance, you might ask members of your community to shoot short videos at church events like picnics, community service projects, special worship services, and so on. Such collaborative video projects can be a particularly effective way to engage the talents and interests of teens and young adults in your community. These videos can be posted on your Facebook page, but they can also be edited together as short montages depicting life in your community. This gets you into the video zone without much scripting or editing effort.

The Reverend Kim Hinrichs and the First Plymouth United Church of Christ in Lincoln, Nebraska, have used video to highlight their music, liturgy, and congregational life.

From there, you can work with staff and other members of your community to create more crafted videos that you share on a YouTube channel for your organization (see below), on Facebook, and on Twitter.

STARTING SIMPLE

If you're uncomfortable diving into video and video editing proper, but are familiar with standard presentation software like PowerPoint and Pages, you can still create short, engaging videos. Elizabeth converted a PowerPoint presentation on *Tweet If You* ♥ *Jesus* into a two-minute trailer for the book. She used vivid photos from her own collection and other royalty-free photos, and added royalty-free music she'd downloaded from iTunes to make for a richer, multimedia experience for viewers.

You can easily convert Power-Point presentations to video by going to the "file" menu and selecting "save as a web movie." For Keynote, you export to a QuickTime movie from the "file" menu.

KEEP IT SHORT, SKIP THE SERMON

Whatever the technology you start with to create your video, you want to make sure to keep it short. In *Enchantment: The Art of Changing Hearts, Minds, and Actions*, Guy Kawasaki writes that "19.4 percent of viewers abandon a video within the first ten

2-MINUTE BIBLE STUDY

In 2010 I launched a new kind of Bible Study—on YouTube. I began it on a whim, but it has become our most popular social media content: a short, sometimes funny, hopefully poignant, personal, bite-sized Biblical reflection.

In the "2-Minute Bible Study" video series, I give a brief reflection on upcoming lectionary readings. The videos appear on our church's YouTube channel, on our website, and on Facebook, and Twitter.

It works for our congregation because it is rooted in scripture and has a liturgical rhythm. As a member said, "It feels like the pastor is right in my living room, talking to me." A newcomer told me, "It was just what I needed to hear, so I came to church today."

2-Minute Bible Study has evolved over time. The first episode was made

Continued

2-MINUTE BIBLE STUDY *Continued*

on my laptop webcam in my office (see page 107). Viewers look up at me, and my head fills the entire frame except for the bright fluorescent lights, drop ceilings, and dark walls.

A Hand Through the Storm
redeemerwoburn 32 videos ⊠ Subscribe

Eventually, we moved into the sanctuary (see above). The camera is a safe distance away and at eye level. You can see the sanctuary interior, with the baptismal font just over my shoulder.

Stained glass illuminates the background. We added music, title slides, and the Bible reference using web-editing software. And I wear a clerical collar, which helps to make clear to viewers that I'm not just some dude with a webcam talking about the Bible.

We're fortunate that we have a member of the congregation with her

Continued

seconds. By sixty seconds, 44 percent have stopped watching. . . . Ensure that your videos are short and sweet and start off with a bang."[6]

That means focusing on one key point, illustrating it as vividly as you can, and connecting with viewers by showing the depth and warmth of your personality. Which is to say: smile and relax. Rather than starting with the generic "Hi, I'm Pastor Sally, and I'd like to talk about Matthew 25 with you today," begin with a captivating statement or question, then introduce yourself. "Ever wonder what the Bible says about investing?" you might ask in a video on stewardship or economic justice.

The short time frame for videos also means that your scintillating sermon on the Beatitudes is not the best material for your foray into video. This is especially true if you read your sermon. Indeed, you want to avoid reading into the camera. You want to have a conversation, so you'll want to practice what you plan to say in advance, perhaps making some notes on key points on large index cards. As we hope has become a clear theme in this book, your digital ministry will be most meaningful, most apt to engage others and invite relationship, when it is most authentically expressive of who you are as a person. Dryly reading from a prepared statement is not going to do that, but it's also the case that over-rehearsing to the point of appearing like a shopping channel huckster is not going to win you any fans either.

It's certainly wonderful if you've got lots to share about your church, organization, and the faith in general. But you'll want to serve that up in bite-sized pieces that people can access from home, work, or while otherwise on the go. Think what you will about short Digital Age attention spans and sound-bite culture, but that's the

2-MINUTE BIBLE STUDY *Continued*

own camera and some background in video editing who has helped us achieve this more highly produced look. But professional production standards are not essential. What's important is that the Gospel reaches as many people as possible in ways they can connect to and engage.

reality of much of life today. It's a reality we have a much greater chance of impacting if, let's say, we offer a two-minute meditation into the midst of an over-scheduled day, than if we insist on blabcasting a twenty-minute sermon.

SETTING UP YOUR YOUTUBE ACCOUNT

To upload a video, you will need a YouTube account. You may recall that the young creators of YouTube became multimillionaires when they sold the site to Google, which means that Steve Chen, Chad Hurley, and Jawed Karim get to zip around the Silicon Valley in very fancy cars and that you can log onto YouTube with your Gmail address. If you don't have a Gmail account, you can quickly set up a YouTube account by clicking on the "create account" option at the top of the YouTube screen. Once you're in, you can begin uploading videos immediately, but you will want to take some time to update your profile, which you can access from the settings menu in the pulldown under your username:

Like Facebook, Twitter, and other social networking sites, YouTube allows you to personalize your account by adding a photo, personal or organizational information, and background formatting. You can actually upload videos before you do any of this, but it's a good idea to invest the twenty minutes or so it will take to set up your account before you upload.

CHANNELS

When you set up your account and select a user name (which can be different from the email address that became your default user name when you signed in), YouTube will prompt you to set up a channel. A YouTube channel is like having your own television station to which you can add videos. A channel keeps all of your ministry videos in one place. Once you've established a channel, you will have a unique web address that will look like this:

http://www.youtube.com/user/Click2SaveBook

From the "settings" tab on your channel, you will be able to develop a fully customized environment that shares basic information about you and your community along with all of your videos:

Channel Tabs

- **Settings**—Create basic information for your site, like tags, name, whether your channel is public or private.
- **Themes and Colors**—Choose from ten different color combinations with the advanced options to customize or create your own. It's a good idea to have your channel match the general look of your website or social media.
- **Modules**—Determine what information is displayed on your channel's pages. This all appears under the videos. It's a good idea to include some of these to help fill out the page and demonstrate activity.
- **Videos and Playlists**—The most important setting determines what content you highlight and display. Choose the featured video— the one people see when they first visit your channel and/or the featured content.

PLAYLISTS

Within your channel, you can create playlists to organize your videos, developing themed content streams within your channel. YouTube creates basic playlists for you automatically: "Favorites," "Liked," "History, "Watch Later."

You can also create your own playlists and assign videos to it. This allows you to express more of your personality and the character of your community by sharing not just videos you've created, but those which you enjoy and value yourself. On the *Click 2 Save* YouTube channel, for example, we've created playlists for videos related to social media, spiritual practices, religious thinkers we admire, and other thought leaders.

A playlist also allows you to get situated in the video landscape before you've been able to complete or upload a video. This is how our playlists functioned before *Click 2 Save* went to press, and we had the time to create a trailer and a couple author videos. The playlists allow us to share insight into who we are as people and some of the background to our thinking before the book is in anyone's hands or on their e-reader.

To create a playlist, choose a video that will go in the playlist. Underneath the video is the link "playlist." Click, and a dropdown menu appears. You can either assign the video to an existing playlist or enter the name of your new playlist and create one.

You can see many of these features at work by visiting the YouTube channel for Keith's church, the Lutheran Church of the Redeemer at *http:// www.youtube.com/user/redeemerwoburn*.

> ## EMBEDDED CODE
>
> YouTube and other video sharing sites typically provide you with a short piece of code that you can place into your blog post or webpage to make the video appear on the page. The code YouTube provides looks like this:
>
> ```
> <iframe width="560" height="315"
> src="http://www.youtube.com/
> embed/8UG9C0G3WSU" frameborder="0"
> allowfullscreen></iframe>
> ```
>
> Copy the code from YouTube. Paste in your HTML editor, and the video should appear. The video continues to be hosted by YouTube, but the code allows it to appear and be played on your site.

UPLOADING VIDEO

Once you've created and edited a video (either live action or from presentation software), it's important to give your video a unique name rather than using the file name automatically generated by your editing software (e.g., "file_43.mov"). Make your titles, descriptions, and the organization of your videos as clear and self-explanatory as possible. While it's great to use humor and wit in your titles, try not to be obscure.

Remember, as we noted earlier, people use YouTube not just as a source for videos, but as a search engine. So, if someone's looking for information on "Protestant sacraments," you don't want to be passed by because your video "Only as Ordained by Christ" seemed more to be about ordination to the priesthood than about the two sacramental rites identified in scripture as required for salvation, baptism and Eucharist. So, include as much information as you can—a title with explanatory subtitle, a short description, tags, description, date, location.

To help with this, YouTube provides some basic editing tools for audio, captions, annotations, and subtitles. The more information you include for your video, account profile, and channel, the easier for people and search engines to find you. Always include your ministry name, location, and your name in the tags, as this is often how people search for congregations. Once you've uploaded one or more videos, you can organize them into channels for your community or personal ministry.

SHARING

The whole point of YouTube, from its inception, is to make video sharing simple. You can share on Facebook, Twitter, Google+, or embed a video on your website. Note, however, rather than posting videos directly to Facebook or Twitter, it's best to post them to YouTube as described here and then share the link to them on Facebook and other sites. This increases the number of views you get directly on YouTube, which moves you up in the YouTube search rankings.

When you share on Facebook and Twitter, be sure to craft a short introduction to the video that shares something of the content—a bit beyond "Here's my latest video!" If you've anchored your video to a provocative question, use the question in your post. "How Does the Bible Speak to Hard Times?" is the theme of a video featuring spiritual writer Barbara Brown Taylor. It's also a great question to pique curiosity about the video.

Our experience is that video is far and away the most anxiety-producing aspect of implementing a social media strategy for most ministry leaders, churches, and other organizations. Those of us raised in the Broadcast Age are used to viewing video the way pre-Reformation believers viewed the Bible: as something best left to the experts. But, affordable, easy-to-use digital cameras and user-friendly editing software have changed all that, allowing almost anyone to become a filmmaker. This ability allows us to share our stories with even more people—especially young adults, who are more drawn to video—and to make our stories more dynamic and engaging.

The good news for even the most cinemographically uncertain is that YouTube gives you the opportunity, through channels and playlists where you host theme-related videos rather than share original ones, to wade into the water a bit. That puts you at the novice level, and from there you can assess your readiness as an individual or organization to move into more customized video-enriched digital ministry practice:

Novice

- Create a YouTube channel
- Complete profile
- Create several playlist categories
- Favorite videos
- Search for other church-related videos to add to your playlist

Oblate

- Create a Keynote or PowerPoint presentation and convert it to video to post on your YouTube channel
- Post a video you already have
- Share your videos and videos from your playlist on your blog, on Facebook, and on Twitter
- Leave comments on other people's videos, inviting viewers to your channel
- Subscribe to the video channels of people whose videos you admire

Superior

- Purchase an inexpensive tripod so your videos are steadier and you can video yourself more easily

- Create a video series or more than one on the same theme
- Use your videos in religious education, formation, spiritual practice, or other church and organizational settings
- Invite members of your congregation or community into the video creation process

3.6 FOURSQUARE

Number of Users	380 million check-ins in 2010
Typical User	• Male, age 25 to 34 • Income over $50,000 • Has 5 to 8 Foursquare friends
Key Features	• Check-ins • Mayorships • Specials • Badges • Integration with Facebook and Twitter
Benefits of Participation	Combines digital and physical presence
Limitations	GPS-enabled smartphone required
Cost	Free

THE BASICS

Nothing communicates value more powerfully in ministry or life than where we put our physical presence. However, outside of worship and the occasional large event, that presence is usually only seen by a few people at a time. Through geolocation social media platforms such as Foursquare, we can use our digital presence in social media to point to our physical presence and tell the story of our ministry. Such digital "check-ins" create a lived map of our ministry that invites those in our networks into deeper relationship.

It's not surprising, after all, that people wonder what ministry leaders do with their time. Much of the work of ministry is hidden as we interact with people one-to-one or in small groups. And much of what we do is confidential. Without revealing personal information, a check-in at a hospital demonstrates something about care to church members and others in need. Check-ins at stops along a youth mission trip help people follow along in real time and communicate the value of service and youth. Check-ins at the neighborhood coffeehouse demonstrate a presence in the local community, much like wearing a digital collar. And these check-ins cue locals in to opportunities to meet you face-to-face.

Jerry Whirtley, pastor at First English Evangelical Lutheran Church in Victoria, Texas, describes the role of check-ins in his ministry this way:

> I check in everywhere I go. It's about community, about how we act as the body of Christ and how, through that, we show other people who Christ is. If I can

interact with somebody because they know where I am, or they can find me more easily because I'm on Twitter or where I check in on Foursquare, then I think I need to do that simply because it allows me to be more accessible to everyone else who might be looking for me or needs to ask me something.

Foursquare is set up as a game, which creates incentives for you to use the service. Each check-in is worth certain point values, and you can compare and compete with your Foursquare friends. If you check in somewhere frequently enough, you can become "the mayor," and, in some cases, receive perks like free coffee at Starbucks. Retailers also sometimes make offers available if you check in at their location.

The game can be a fun. For ministry, however, the game is not nearly as important as the story Foursquare enables you to tell. Foursquare is good for:

- Answering questions like, "What do ministry leaders do beyond Sunday morning?"
- Using your digital presence to point to your physical presence
- Documenting travel related to ministry, such as mission trips
- Connecting with people locally, if they share their location
- Sharing your ministry in real time

Because the Foursquare network is relatively small, and Foursquare members have fewer connections, its main value is as a central check-in tool across social media networks like Facebook and Twitter.

SETTING UP YOUR FOURSQUARE ACCOUNT

Foursquare is used as a mobile application on a smartphone. Download the Foursquare app to your GPS-enabled smartphone. If you join on your home computer, you'll be prompted to enroll through your Facebook account. This will allow you to coordinate Foursquare and Facebook check-ins automatically.

When you download the Foursquare mobile app, you'll be asked to enter an email address and password. Once you've entered your account information, select "check-in" and you will see a list of locations near you. Select the location where you want to check in and the social networks on which you want to share it. When you check in you can leave tips about the location and share photos.

Check-ins can tell a great story in a small space, combining maps, pictures, comments, and links with the places you visit. Here's how the same check-in looks when shared on Facebook and Twitter:

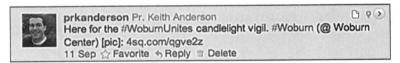

On Facebook, people can click the location for more information and view pictures, maps, and comments from others who have checked in there. If he's tweeting, Keith includes the common hashtags of #Woburn for his town. He added the #WoburnUnites hashtag for a candlelight vigil held after the manhunt discussed in section 3.2:

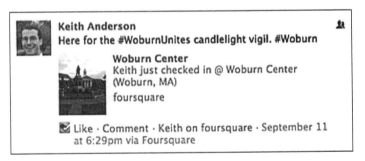

Revealing your real-time location does raise privacy concerns. Foursquare offers a range of privacy options. With any check-in you can selectively share your location with some combination of Foursquare friends, Facebook friends, on Twitter, or none of these. It depends on your comfort level and what you are trying to accomplish. If you're connecting with a local community or colleagues, you could establish yourself by sharing your whereabouts on Twitter. Just keep in mind that any information you share in any social network can be shared by others.

You might start by checking in to the places where it's publicly known you will be. For instance, check in to church on Sunday morning or at a public hearing on a matter of deep concern to your organization.

Facebook also features a check-in option. The advantage of Facebook check-ins is that you can tag other Facebook users. And, you're already registered if you're a Facebook user, so there's no new profile to set up. The downside is that it's only viewable on Facebook. Like videos posted on YouTube and then shared on Facebook, using Foursquare creates another web property, expanding your presence and providing one more way others can connect with you and your ministry.

FOURSQUARE VENUES

Foursquare also allows you to claim and manage venues (the places where people check in). Just about every address listing you'd find in the phone book is already included in Foursquare, so your church is likely already there. Go on the Foursquare website and search for your ministry site. Select the option to claim your listing and become the manager. Add information like pictures and a description. This creates more interest for people checking in. When they check in and share with their social networks, their friends in those networks can see information about your church along with engaging photos.

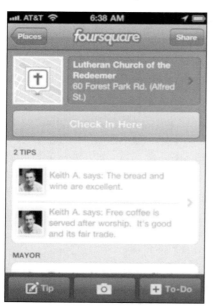

Encourage others to check in and thereby publicize your location. Putting a Foursquare sticker on your door, the Foursquare icon on your website, or a reminder in the bulletin will help to generate interest.

Be sure to add content to your venue over time. Keith checks in on Foursquare every Sunday morning when he arrives at church. He includes a picture of something in the sanctuary, and a little text about the themes for the morning. This share also appears on Facebook and Twitter. All of this gives life to the venue page.

Like LinkedIn, Foursquare is a social media experience in which fewer people tend to participate—but it is growing. And, as with all of the other major platforms, it's important that you build some level of participation into your strategy. As you begin (or extend) your digital ministry, having a Foursquare novitiate is probably sufficient. But you'll want to spend time thinking through the ways that other levels of participation can help your church or organization to extend a wider welcome and how you can make your ministry presence known outside your doors:

Novice

- Create a profile with picture
- Link to your Facebook and Twitter profiles
- Find a Foursquare role model among your friends
- Check in to a few places to get the hang of it

Oblate

- Claim your church or organization as a Foursquare venue
- Add information to your venue profile

Superior

- Check in everywhere you go in relation to your ministry, but be selective about how you will share your check-ins
- Do a "week in the life of a pastor"
- Check in to your home venue and include pictures and tips, if appropriate. When people visit your venue, they will see a robust community.

DIGITAL MINISTRY STRATEGY: BUILD YOUR SOCIAL MEDIA PLATFORM

The following steps are designed to help you build a digital social media platform based on your particular ministry context, the people you hope to reach, and the story you wish to tell. It's most effective if you gather input from your community as you work through the steps below.

1. **Prioritize.** Given your ministry setting, the network of relationships you hope to develop, and available time, rank the following social media featured in this chapter in order of priority:

Social Media	High	Medium	Low
Facebook	❏	❏	❏
Twitter	❏	❏	❏
LinkedIn	❏	❏	❏
Blog	❏	❏	❏
YouTube	❏	❏	❏
Foursquare	❏	❏	❏

2. **Build Your Platform.** Your high priority social media communities will make up the core of your digital ministry presence, where you will develop and share the heart of your story. Apply the following questions to each of your top three platforms. As you become more proficient in these, you may want to add other platforms to your digital ministry portfolio. But, complete Step 3 below—assessment—before you revise your strategy.

Platform A: _____

With whom do you hope to connect?

_____

_____

_____

What story do you wish to tell about your faith, your ministry, your community, or your life more generally?

_____

_____

_____

What techniques and/or examples from the chapter will help you tell that story?

_____

_____

_____

Who might you consider as role models on this platform as you develop your own digital ministry practice?*

_____

_____

_____

Platform B: _____

With whom do you hope to connect?

_____

_____

_____

---

* Everyone we interviewed for the book is active on Facebook or Twitter—usually both. Don't be shy about following people on Twitter, subscribing to the public Facebook profile, and connecting with them on other social networks to learn more about their approach to digital ministry. Different people have different approaches to accepting new Facebook friends, following back, or otherwise personally connecting with people they don't know from face-to-face engagements or professional introductions. But we included them in the book—and they agreed to be interviewed—because they have much to share about digital ministry. Learn all you can as you observe them in their various social media habitats.

What story do you wish to tell about your faith, your ministry, your community, or your life more generally?

_____

_____

_____

What techniques and/or examples from the chapter will help you tell that story?

_____

_____

_____

Who might you consider as role models on this platform as you develop your own digital ministry practice?

_____

_____

_____

Platform C: _____

With whom do you hope to connect?

_____

_____

_____

What story do you wish to tell about your faith, your ministry, your community, or your life more generally?

_____

_____

_____

What techniques and/or examples from the chapter will help you tell that story?

_____

_____

_____

Who might you consider as role models on this platform as you develop your own digital ministry practice?

_____

_____

_____

3. **Assess Engagement and Impact.** The mega-church movement, and American culture in general, has impressed upon us the idea that "more is better"—more friends, more followers, more platforms, more members. But the key measures in digital media are not numerical, but relational. The questions below will help you to assess meaningful ministry engagement in each platform. Consider reviewing this assessment on a quarterly basis and making adjustments to your strategy in consultation with your social media and local communities.

What specific stories illustrate how each platform has helped to engage with members of your local church or faith community?

_____

_____

_____

What specific stories illustrate how each platform has helped to engage with people in your area who are _not_ members of your faith community?

_____

_____

_____

What specific stories illustrate how each platform has helped to engage with people from different social or demographic groups than those usually represented in your community?

_____

_____

_____

What specific stories illustrate how each platform has helped to connect with people outside of your area professionally, spiritually, or otherwise?

_____

_____

_____

How much time do you now spend on digital ministry?

_____ Minutes a Day _____ Minutes a Week

Is this too much or too little in light of the engagement and impact you've observed?

_____

_____

_____

How might expanding to other platforms help your ministry? Again, more isn't necessarily better. How will connecting with new social networks help you to extend God's love, fellowship, and compassion to others? How might it take away from other aspects of your ministry?

_____

_____

_____

4. **Next Steps.** Based on your quarterly assessment, what specific practices will you (and your community) take to deepen your networked, relational, incarnational digital ministry?

❏ None. Staying the course and getting more proficient where I/we are seems like the best approach right now.

❏ Deeper practice in current platforms. I/we will work on connecting more with people in our current networks in the following ways:

_____

_____

_____

❏ Adding new networks. I/we will start developing networks in order to extend our story and connect more widely.

❏ Pulling back from networks in order to focus time and attention more fully where I/we seem to be having the most engagement and impact.

4

PRACTICING THE ARTS
OF DIGITAL MINISTRY

 Digital ministry isn't just about the new spaces into which we extend our ministry in the Digital Age. It's also about how we adapt basic practices of ministry to these spaces. In this chapter, we explore the ministry arts of offering hospitality, caring for God's people, forming disciples, building community, and making public witness as these practices play out in social networking communities and as they're shaped by social digital culture. In the final section of the chapter, we share three profiles of ministry leaders who have effectively adapted these practices in the context of digital ministry.

DIGITAL MINISTRY CALLS US INTO NEW SPACES and invites us to develop new relationships with people from our own communities, with neighbors we may never otherwise have known, and with those who might never step inside our churches or organizations. But the newness of our participation in digital spaces can sometimes obscure the fact that we rely on very basic, indeed, very traditional modes of engaging that have served us well for generations. In the Introduction, we revisited these core practices though the LACE model that Elizabeth presented in *Tweet If You ♥ Jesus*:

- *Listening*—taking time to get to know people in social networks based on what they share in profiles, posts, tweets, and so on, rather than making communicating your message the priority
- *Attending*—noticing and being present to the experiences and interests of others as they share themselves in digital spaces

- *Connecting*—Reaching out to others in diverse communities in order to deepen and extend the networks that influence your digital spiritual practice
- *Engaging*—building relationships by sharing content, collaborating, and connecting people to others

These basic practices allow people of faith to enter digital communities from a networked, relational perspective, with the goal of getting to know others in a more sustained way over time and connecting more deeply within and across communities. This contrasts with what amounts to a marketing effort aimed at getting a message to as many people as possible without regard to who they are as particular persons in community. The LACE model is the starting point for meaningful relationship in the digitally integrated world.

But for those who are engaged more specifically in serving and attending God's people wherever they are, participating in digital communities calls for distinctive ministry practices. This vocational distinction has nothing, of course, to do with status or rank. Rather, it has to do with being present very clearly as servants of God's people in digital spaces, much in the way that ordained ministers wear collars in local spaces so that people see and understand their vocational calling. Lay ministers distinguish themselves in other ways—through profile descriptions that name lay ministries, for instance— but as with clergy, they also make themselves available to people for specific kinds of engagement meant to enrich the lives of others and invite them into deeper relationship with God.

In this chapter, we have included five specific arts of ministry that bring Christian belief, tradition, and action into conversation with the spiritual dimensions of everyday life as they are encountered in digital and physical spaces. These digital ministry arts—each of which incorporates listening, attending, connecting, and engaging in concrete ways—are as follows:

- *Offering Hospitality*—Creating sacred space and welcoming others into it
- *Caring for God's People*—Sharing prayer, encouragement, inspiration, and wisdom
- *Forming Disciples*—Enriching spiritual lives through education, small group practice, and preaching
- *Building Community*—Connecting within and across local and digital networks and connecting others to those with complementary interests

- *Making Public Witness*—Bearing witness to the love of God in Jesus Christ through words and actions so that others are inspired and invited to experience this love; and advocating for and encouraging action that advances the just reign of God

We might have included any number of other ministry arts, such as worship, sacramental ministries, formal spiritual direction, or vocational mentoring. And, there are those who would argue, not without merit, that preaching could easily be called out as a separate category that combines formation, witness, and proclamation. As we noted in Chapter 3, preaching is, as a genre, not always particularly well-suited to digital spaces, and our observation has been that it invites a certain over-messaging among those whose offline ministries involve a good deal of preaching. For this reason, and because of the practical demand that we narrow the list of practices we explore, we limited our discussion of preaching to its role in formation.

We narrowed our list not only because of the limits of space within this book, but also because we are keen to situate digital ministry across the often rigidly conceived boundaries between the laity and the ordained. Among the great gifts of digital social media communities are the opportunities they present to members of what Protestants refer to as "the priesthood of all believers" to explore and share their faith and to develop their own vocations as ministers in the church, formally or as affirmed by the people they serve.

As we considered the arts of digital ministry in this light, we wanted to focus on those that would tend to avoid the complexities and conflicts about what constitutes lay and ordained ministry "proper." Beyond this, our bias throughout this book has been to focus on ministry practices that enrich and extend face-to-face worship and community rather than advocating for those which research has shown tend to compete with face-to-face spiritual relationships and communities. This contributed to the more limited treatment of preaching, and also to our decision not to include worship practices or sacramental ministries, though these are certainly to be found in digital spaces.[1]

The sections that follow describe these arts and offer brief examples of digital ministers who have effectively included them in their digital practice. The final sections of the chapter offer three more detailed narratives exploring the practice of digital ministry by Lutheran pastor Nadia Bolz-Weber, Episcopal priest Matthew Moretz, and by the Massachusetts Council of Churches and its executive director, Laura Everett.

4.1 OFFERING HOSPITALITY: THE DIGITAL NARTHEX

Where does hospitality begin? For many churches it happens just inside the front door. There, in the narthex, or entryway, greeters wait to welcome members and newcomers to worship. Visitor packets stuffed with information are stacked near the door. Guest books and visitor cards wait to be filled out. Ushers hand out worship materials and help people to their pews.

These are certainly good practices of welcoming. The problem, of course, is that only the people who show up for church get to experience this hospitality. What's more, even those who come through our church doors can often get the impression that they only exist for us once they fill out a visitor card. Often, our welcome is more of an introduction of us than an embrace of the visitor, whether or not she or he plans to come back again.

Today, digital social media enable congregations to extend hospitality and welcome beyond the front door into digital spaces. And, not unimportantly, digital culture demands this. Rather than passively waiting for people to walk through our doors, ministry leaders and congregations must be more active and visibly participatory in social media communities—making ourselves available, greeting strangers, finding points of connection, and creating what we might call a digital narthex. But the relational emphasis of social networking sites also presses us to connect in ways that move well

---

HOSPITALITY AND RECIPROCITY

Much of what we and other digital ministers admire has to do with how we open our digital spaces—church and personal Facebook pages, Twitter feeds, etc.—to others. That's certainly important. But it's also important to remember that the world doesn't revolve around our social media presence. Everyone with whom we might want to connect, whom we might want to engage, who might need the ministry we hope to share, isn't going to randomly happen into our digital neighborhood. It's important, then, to get out a bit. Visit other people's personal and group Facebook pages, leaving messages of friendship, encouragement, and support. Leave comments on online news sites, and include a link to your Twitter feed or your organization's Facebook page.

Perhaps most importantly, share the digital love by following people back when they follow you on Twitter, by liking others' Facebook group pages, and by friending people you

Continued

HOSPITALITY *Continued*

meet as often as you wait for others to friend you. Nothing says "I only care about you when you're listening to me" like a Twitter user who has a thousand followers, but only follows a couple dozen chosen few. Nothing says "You're only important when you have something for me" like sharing content someone else has posted without giving them credit by name.

Hospitality is not just a matter of opening your digital door, but of being willing to travel across the digital domain on a regular basis. Digital hospitality depends on reciprocity—taking the kinds of walks, even out of our comfort zones, that Jesus called us to as disciples and which the apostles and saints modeled.

beyond the visitor card and brochures about church programs we tend to dole out at the front door.

WHY A WEBSITE WELCOME IS NOT ENOUGH

Websites can certainly provide a measure of hospitality, particularly if they express an attentiveness to the needs of visitors and newcomers, help to tell an engaging story of your ministry, and paint a picture of what someone might expect at worship or other public gatherings. However, websites are simply not enough. Websites, although they increasingly integrate elements of social media, are really primarily about providing information.

Thanks to the search engine Google, people have more than enough information about most of the basics of your church or organization—and often much deeper detail as well—right at their fingertips. In fact, they often have too much. Some have even said we are suffering from "information fatigue." Information provided on a website is important for people who want to know the who, what, when, and where of your community, but it is no substitute for active and authentic attending and connecting as ministry leaders. People don't need more information. What they want is relationship—with you, with your community, and with others like them who are beginning to explore their faith in a new setting. To the extent that your website can point them to that sort of experience by connecting people to your Facebook community, for instance, or highlighting YouTube videos that bring more of your story to life, your website is a valuable part of your social media strategy. But it's hardly the whole digital ministry enchilada.

@KLAMACH COMES TO CHURCH

Keith's congregation had a particularly powerful experience of the effect of hospitality in digital spaces on participation in local spaces when Chris Lawrence, whom Keith had met through Twitter, visited the church for Sunday services. Lawrence (@klamach) is a spiritual seeker. Part of his search has taken place on Twitter, where he became connected to the Church and Social Media tweetchat (#chsocm) we discussed earlier, in which Keith regularly participates. In a common social media story of unfolding and deepening connection, Chris and Keith became aware of one another, had some casual engagement, passed a few questions back and forth—in this case, on Lutheran worship. All of this eventually led to Chris's visit to the Lutheran Church of Redeemer.

Chris tweeted about his experience afterwards:

 klamach Chris Lawrence
#Awesome and holy experience worshipping with @prkanderson this morning! I read 2 of the prayers!
23 Oct

And, Keith tweeted back his own gratitude for Lawrence's participation:

 prkanderson Pr. Keith Anderson
Thanks for praying! RT @klamach: The Prayers of Intercession I read/lead this morning at Redeemer yfrog.com/odlz4cj
23 Oct

Lawrence's blog post added more depth to the experience. "I found myself this morning at a church where, just a mere four months ago," he wrote, "I never would have imagined myself worshipping."

The experience of hospitality and welcome that brought Chris to Redeemer that Sunday played out on Twitter 140 characters at a time over the course of a few weeks. But even this slight gesture opened a conversation and bridged what was clearly a yawning spiritual gap for Chris.

DIGITAL MONASTIC HOSPITALITY: AS IF THEY WERE CHRIST

The monastic Rule of St. Benedict has, for centuries, guided the lives not only of those who join monastic communities, but also of many who seek to live their faith according to a clear and balanced appreciation of the teachings of Christ as they apply to the very practical demands of everyday life. The Benedictine Rule highlights, in particular, the spiritual significance of hospitality in its instruction with regard to the reception of guests:

> All guests who arrive should be received as if they were Christ, for He himself is going to say: "I came as a stranger, and you received Me"; and let due honor be shown to all, especially those who share our faith and those who are pilgrims.[2]

The monks of the Society of Saint John the Evangelist, an Episcopal monastery in Cambridge, Massachusetts, are greatly influenced by the Benedictine Rule. Their own more contemporary Rule of Life brings the monastic practice of hospitality into digital communities as well as anyone we've seen. Through Facebook, Twitter, blogs, Flickr, and YouTube, these "monks for a new century" open the monastic enclosure to the world, offering the gifts of the monastic tradition, and inviting visitors to engage with the life of the community through pictures, sermons, gems of monastic wisdom, audio and written reflections—all of which make monastic life accessible, visible, and engaging for new generations of seekers. People can feel a part of the community before they walk in the doors, and those who cannot or may not ever have the opportunity to walk through the doors can still find comfort, encouragement, and inspiration.

The community's Flickr stream shows a vibrant, diverse, and evolving community at worship, at prayer, dining, working, and celebrating together over time, across natural and liturgical seasons, and through important changes in the community, like an extensive renovation of the monastery. While many of these photos can also be accessed through the SSJE website, the monks take care to be present elsewhere in digital landscape so that their welcome is available to travelers on Flickr, Facebook, Twitter, and YouTube. This makes invitation, hospitality, welcome, and relationship an ongoing possibility—an act of will, or providence, or grace.

CREATING DIGITAL SACRED SPACE

This practice of digital hospitality has the effect of creating sacred space within the digital landscape. As Kimberly Knight, a minister of the United Church of Christ and co-pastor of Koinonia Church of the virtual reality community Second Life, says, "What makes it a sacred space is being able to honor who is there." We do that through a ministry presence which incorporates noticing, accepting, and reaching out in kindness and compassion to the others in our midst. Whenever we receive one another in Christian love, in digital or face-to-face locales, we can suddenly see that we are standing together in spaces made sacred by our very connection.

Sacred space in social media can be found in multiple forms. It can be found in designated places like a monastery Facebook page, blogs with spiritual reflection, or a Twitter stream dedicated to prayer and inspiration. Like church sanctuaries, these are places where it is commonly understood that God is present and the purpose of gathering is to be attentive to that presence. For example, the Abbey of the Arts Facebook page, maintained by writer, spiritual director, and Benedictine oblate Christine Valters Paintner, serves as a quiet place for shared contemplation and reflection within the bustle of the digital world. On it, Paintner offers inspirational quotes, spiritual commentary, and online classes that "support the integration of contemplative practice, expressive arts, and an awareness of nature's rhythms."

While Paintner's Abbey of the Arts website offers far more extensive resources, including her remarkable photographs and poetry, the Facebook page has a dailiness to it that allows it to function not just as a spiritual resource, but as a sacred space for people who have connected through Paintner's workshops or spiritual direction ministry, or who know her and those

in her extended community only through her writing, visual art, and facilitation of spiritual conversation. Such spaces serve as spiritual oases—reminders that the divine is always in our midst, made known to us through our connectedness to one another and all of creation.

DIGITAL SANCTUARY: SENDING KIRSTIN TO GOD

The sacred potential of digital space is perhaps nowhere more pointed than in the increasing number of Facebook memorial pages that have begun to emerge over the past few years. We may be aware of ones for celebrities like pop icon Michael Jackson or in the case of tragedies like the suicide of Tyler Clementi, the Rutgers student whose roommate leaked a video of him kissing a man. These pages allow for a collective expression of grief and loss and seem to serve as outlets for expressions of the confusion, anger, and anguish that accompany both death and cultural change. And, certainly, it is appropriate for ministry leaders—people trained and experienced in helping others to deal with loss—to participate in such spaces.

But another kind of memorial page has also developed in digital spaces, a kind which connects the personal to the communal and, especially at the end of life, the temporal to the eternal. For instance, through the spring and summer of 2011, a digital sanctuary began to form on the Facebook page of Kirstin Paisley, a lay minister to the homeless, a blogger, a friend to many, and a young woman who was dying of cancer.

Kirstin had been fighting cancer for years, narrating the story of hope and struggle on her blog, *Barefoot and Laughing*, and connecting through this digital ministry to people around the world who were inspired by her honesty, her vulnerability, and her remarkable good humor in the face of so great an ongoing challenge.

When it became clear in the summer that the treatment regimen, which itself had been something of a torment, was not holding the cancer at bay, Kirstin shared the news on her blog and on her Facebook page. She let people know how much they meant to her and how much she wanted them to be with her as she returned to God.

In the weeks after Kirstin's painful, but characteristically hopeful, announcement, her Facebook page became a gathering place for prayer, reflection, gestures of comfort, and love that one would be hard-pressed to call "superficial" in any way. People held vigil with Kirstin on the night she died and prayed around the clock and around the world with those tending to her at home.

"It was remarkable," says the Reverend Andee Zetterbaum, who cared for Kirstin at the end of her life, including helping to maintain her Facebook page and update her blog. "People were so spiritually present on the page, and I know that meant so much to Kirstin. She really felt surrounded by the whole communion of saints as she left this life. It was an unbelievable comfort not just to Kirstin, but maybe even more to those of us who had to let her go."

This "letting go" extended beyond Facebook. Zetterbaum, as she had promised Kirstin, updated the blog as Kirstin became less able to communicate. When Kirstin died on the first day of July, Zetterbaum shared the news on the blog:

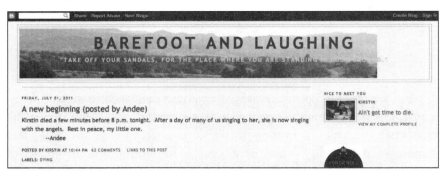

When members of Kirstin's far-flung digital community expressed a desire to be part of the memorial service for Kirstin, Zetterbaum enlisted the help of another friend, Sean McConnell, the Canon for Communications in the Episcopal Diocese of California, who videotaped the service and

posted it on the video hosting site Vimeo, with links from the blog and Facebook. Social media thus enabled people in a widely distributed community to gather in love and hope.

The separation and privatization that characterized modern culture after the printing press and, more so, the Industrial Revolution and the birth of broadcast media, rendered dying, death, and mourning profoundly private, often socially disconnected experiences. Moreover, modernity, with its emphasis on very specific spaces for every life function—birth, education, work, worship, and death—forced an artificial separation between what we came to know as "the sacred" and the "profane," or ordinary spaces in our lives. But Kirstin Paisley insisted that all of the people in her life— those known to her from face-to-face experience, and those known only from digital engagement—mattered in every moment of her life. This allowed them to be active, compassionate participants even in her death, calling forth the sacredness of her life, of their common experience, and of the digital spaces where their relationships often developed.

VIMEO

Like YouTube, Vimeo is a video-sharing site where you can upload, share, and view videos. It is a much smaller network, with just over three million members compared to YouTube's 490 million unique users.

Though your video is less likely to go viral on the site, Vimeo is preferred by many because it does not have advertisements (yet) and because it allows users to upload longer videos.

For more on using video in your digital ministry, see Chapter 3.6 about YouTube.

It is perhaps no small wonder, then, that Kirstin's Facebook page continues to be something of a sanctuary. Friends remember her birthday in September, and stop by from time to time to share memories of their experience with her, prayers for and to her, and, increasingly, to offer welcome to other people dealing with cancer to whom Kirstin's living and dying remain a potent model of faith and hope.

"Kirsten, thank you for helping me find the right words to say to my grandmother who is so very scared to die," writes one recent visitor to the page who was inspired by one of Kirstin's many stories. "I told her the story about you and the cardinal. Even after passing into the next, you and your life still help minister to those in need."

And, recognizing the sanctity of the digital space that held so much meaning in Kirstin's life, Zetterbaum continues to minister to people who visit. "Kirstin created this amazing network," she says. "I don't really know most of these people outside of the Facebook page or the blog, but I know how much they meant to Kirstin and how much they mean to one another now. It's hard to turn away from that as a priest."

DIGITAL LIMINALITY

Sacred space also becomes apparent to us in less clearly defined, perhaps more random, ways across the social media landscape through the countless sacred moments of deep understanding, the acknowledgement of our common humanity, the sharing of our hopes, and the vulnerability and intimacy we express as we wrestle with our faith and doubt, and seek to heal our brokenness in community. In the welcome and love of others, in reciprocal appreciation, we glimpse our inestimable value to God. These moments pop up all over the digital world, as people connect and engage in ways they might never do in a church or other religious organization.

Sometimes these moments may seem insignificant. A birthday greeting is offered to a Facebook "friend" we may not know at all in person. Someone "likes" a photo you've posted of your kid's first day of school. An almost stranger comments in the perfect way on a tweet or Facebook status update. It can seem like nothing sometimes, these small social media gestures. Yet time and again we learn how much they mean to people, how significant they are in the context of daily lives whose challenges and complexity are largely invisible to us. In this way, digital locales often appear to be not unlike the "thin places" of pre-Christian and Celtic tradition, where the line between creation and the divine, the temporal and the eternal, seems less sharply drawn, where we seem able to be more present to God and God to us.

"Liminal spaces," theologians often call these locales and the experience of a spiritual "in-between" that seems possible there. This is, of course, exactly where Jesus asked the apostles and the disciples who followed in their footsteps to go when he called them—and calls us—to share the Good News with "the whole of creation" (Mark 16:15). We are called to walk among the people, and in doing so, to progressively trample down the barriers that keep us all from knowing the Kingdom that Jesus promises us is always near. This liminal possibility is richly present in social media communities when we open ourselves to the matrix of networks and relationships available there. In doing so, we claim the digital landscape as sacred space, a locale where the grace of Jesus Christ, the love of God, and the fellowship of the Holy Spirit (2 Cor. 13:13) is as present as it is in our churches, our homes, our workplaces, our schools, and everywhere else in our physical communities.

4.2 Caring for God's People: Logging In to Digital Ministry

It is a paradox of social media that people will share very intimate and some-times life-and-death matters in social media spaces, even as such sharing immediately becomes both public and permanent. Today, new loves, break-ups, engagements, marriages, divorces, birth and death announcements, health news, and personal locations are all shared online.

Social media can serve as a good "leading indicator" that something is amiss with someone. People share that they've had a hard day, that one of the kids is sick, that dinner was a disaster. They post expressions of grief, news about changes in jobs and relationships. Even updates about lousy weather or political frustrations give us insight into the lives of people in our local and extended communities. When we login, pay attention, and listen with heart and mind as people share their lives, we often become aware of things we may not have otherwise discovered.

FOR WHOM SHALL WE NOW PRAY?

This kind of open and generous sharing calls us to deep listening and prayer. Indeed, digital ministers recognize that their Facebook news feeds and Twitter streams are places of and occasions for prayer.

Sister Heather Rollins, OPA, the "Undercover Nun" you met in Chapter 3, is a member of the Anglican Order of Preachers. She describes prayer in the context of her digital ministry and her vocation more generally this way: "On Twitter, if I see a prayer request come up, I pray. People will say 'thank you,' and I'll say, 'you're welcome.' But I'm a sister, it's what we do. It's my job."

Depending on the sentiments or needs expressed, digital ministers can comment, direct message, email, call, or visit in person. Facebook also makes it easy to mark milestones like birthdays and anniversaries, changes in rela-tionship status, new jobs, or a move to a new home. People deeply appreciate these digital expressions of pastoral attentiveness and concern.

This is one area where ministers can sometimes save time through social media. Many life updates that have traditionally been received at the sanctu-ary door after church are now being shared online. Leaving an expression of concern, care, and support can sometimes save a phone call or having to track someone down at church on Sunday. So, for all the worries we often hear about social media creating another ministry "time suck," it is often a valuable time saver.

More importantly, such digital ministry gestures through the week are more immediate and more closely connected to the news as it has played out in a person's life. When we take a few seconds to check in, we show our attentiveness to members of our community, whether they belong to our church or organization or not.

We can also actively solicit prayer requests, a common practice for Presbyterian minister and popular San Francisco Bay Area blogger Bruce Reyes-Chow. Reyes-Chow is in the habit, both on his Facebook page and on Twitter, of calling people to prayer. "For whom shall we now pray?" he will post, and his robust band of friends and followers will offer up their concerns into a widely distributed digital network, their prayers reaching out to one another and to all of their networks as witness to their faith and their connection to each other. All this, on the basis of a mere twenty-seven tweetable characters plucked out, most of the time, on Reyes-Chow's smartphone as he travels hither and yon in his ministry.

Reyes-Chow also often offers more focused prayers that both speak to his own concerns and invite the community that gathers on his Facebook page and Twitter feed into conversation about important questions of meaning in contemporary life. During the Penn State sexual abuse scandal in the fall of 2011, for instance, Reyes-Chow shifted the conversation considerably by praying on Facebook and Twitter ". . . for those who experience abuse, brokenness and rejection, and then are forced to relive it all again. Lord hear our prayers."

LIFTING ONE ANOTHER UP

Other ministry leaders orient their social media participation toward encouragement and inspiration. As part of his morning devotions, for instance, the Roman Catholic bishop of Indianapolis, Christopher Coyne, posts prayers, reflections, and information about special observances, as well as a prayer of the day (POD) and quote of the day (QOD):

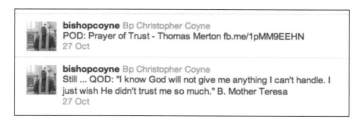

Coyne also shares his own reflections on the readings for the day:

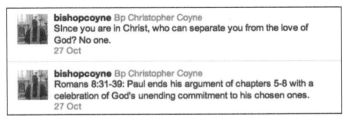

Bishop Coyne does not just tweet and leave it at that. He actively engages with Twitter followers, discussing the relative merits of the @DivineOffice Twitter feed over the iBreviary application for the iPhone and participating from time to time in the weekly Church and Social Media (#chsocm) tweetchat. He answers questions about the faith, translates Latin phrases, explains customs and traditions, and generally helps to make the faith more visible and accessible not only to Catholics, but to a diverse network of followers.

AFFIRMING THE SACRED IN THE ORDINARY: CHEESES SAVE

Beyond critical moments and milestones of people's lives, we can also bear witness to how people are living their ministries in daily life.

One of the common critiques of social networking is that people are just sharing a bunch of mundane stuff. Well, kind of. And, yet, this is all part of their holy calling. The Protestant Reformations shifted the seat of vocation from the spiritual elite to everyone—from the priesthood of some to the priesthood of all. It claimed the holy in the midst of all the stuff of everyday life. So, too, the post-Vatican II Roman Catholic Church has affirmed the baptismal call of all believers to minister as disciples of Christ, whether in lay or ordained roles, in the church, the home, the community, and the workplace.

Among the most meaningful things digital ministers can do is name their relationships, their parenting, their work, and their volunteering, with all the associated joys and struggles, as expressions of their faith—as the holy action of disciples. Such quotidian sanctity can be called out in digital communities in ways that are often not possible in face-to-face settings. For instance, one rarely sees someone stand up at a local coffee shop—and we might worry if we did—to announce that she is praying for her ailing aunt or that he just witnessed an amazing act of kindness and generosity between a corporate drone and a homeless person on a busy downtown street.

"I think we can all agree that cheese is sacred," posts a member of the Episcopal Foodie Network page on Facebook, sharing with the quip the true holiness of our food preparation and meal sharing practices. Such posts on individual and group pages insist on the sacred possibility of all creation—digital and physical—and they witness to a Christian understanding of ordinary holiness that nuances considerably the extreme characterizations of Christians in most broadcast media.

However, the language of affirmation does not have to be overtly religious. Our very presence can communicate God's own presence and care. We can, as Paul wrote to the Romans, "rejoice with those who rejoice, and weep with those who weep" (Rom. 12:15). By our presence, we can point to God's presence in joys and heartache, in the mundane and the sublime. This is far less dramatic than moments of spiritual crisis, but, over the long term, this is how pastoral relationships are built and tended, whether by ordained or lay digital ministers.

It turns out that one of the biggest critiques of social media is actually one of its greatest gifts: the brevity of digital engagement usually offers quite enough space to celebrate small blessings throughout everyday life, to share mustard seeds of faith as we comment, "like," tweet, retweet, and so on with the people of God who wander through the digital landscape during the big and small moments of their lives.

4.3 FORMING DISCIPLES: LEARNING IN COMMUNITY

Social media is changing the way we learn because it has changed the way we access information and the way we connect with one another. Scott McLeod, a professor of educational leadership at the University of Kentucky, describes it this way: "We no longer live in an information push-out world where we passively receive information that is broadcast out to us by large, centralized entities. Instead, we now live within multi-directional conversation spaces."[3]

The ability people have to find out about almost anything on Google, Wikipedia, or YouTube necessarily changes the role of the ministry leader as educator. Clergy and lay educators no longer function as "resident theologians" by virtue of any special *gnosis* received in seminary or from the shelves of theological books in their offices. They are no longer seen as repositories of information. Rather, in a sea of information, they help others to become theologians themselves, inviting people to reflect critically upon all the information they encounter and to engage that information more deeply through conversation with others. Digital ministers, then, facilitate relationships between people and information rather than imparting information as all-knowing fonts of wisdom. Says Michael Wesch, the Carnegie Foundation's National Teacher of the Year in 2008, "I like to think that we are not teaching subjects but subjectivities: ways of approaching, understanding, and interacting with the world."[4] This relational knowing is as significant for the church as it is for any other part of society today.

Just as websites are not a substitute for hospitality, posting sermons or adult education materials on a blog are not substitutes for formation. A sermon or educational blog is a good service to provide for those unable to attend church on Sunday or those who missed the most recent event with your organization. It can also be a helpful way to learn the practice of blogging. (Indeed, it's how both Keith and Elizabeth got started with social media.) However, it should not be mistaken for a form of engagement. That, says Darleen Pryds, a professor of church history at the Franciscan School of Theology in Berkeley, California, is "a very middle-aged approach to social media." Although she is a medievalist, Pryds is not talking here about media in the Middle Ages, but about a way of seeing social media merely as faster, cheaper tools for broadcasting a message to more people—an approach that tends to characterize those of us "of a certain age" who were not raised with media that facilitated social engagement.

FORMATION ON TAP

Consider, for example, the difference between traditional parish adult education classes and the increasingly popular "theology pubs" offered by churches, seminaries, and other religious organizations. In a traditional adult education class, people gather in the church building to hear a priest, pastor, or lay educator impart information. There may be discussion—some of it in fact quite lively—but the structure of the learning engagement will generally be fairly clearly centered on the teacher who doles out information and questions to the students.

By contrast, at a theology pub, a guest or resident theologian facilitates conversation around the table, and everyone's perspective brings something meaningful to the discussion of, for instance, what incarnation means in the Digital Age, or maybe how grace functions in the lives of postmodern believers. This ranging conversation happens out in the open, in public—the world is not "out there," an abstraction. It is all around. It is open to and engaged with it. This is the same kind of formation that happens in social media: a theological conversation happening in a public place, influenced by life all around it, overheard and overseen, as words like "God," "Jesus," and "shalom" leaven the life around it. The world of faith is not imagined or enacted as something separate from the world of pub-goers and workers and honking car horns. It is all right there.

Two dangers of online formation are that learning can become individualized—between "me and my Bible" or "me and my computer"—and that people can seek out only those who reinforce their ideas, rather than challenge or qualify them. This can happen, of course, in traditional classroom learning settings as well, where students have been trained over time to see learning as an exchange between "me and the teacher" or "me and the book." Like many other practices developed through the modern era, and especially in the Broadcast Age, approaches to learning that highlight the expertise or celebrity of a teacher and amplify the separateness and relative anonymity of learners tend to reinforce many of the most individualistic characteristics of modern culture. It's all about me and what I'm "getting out of" a particular educational session.

CONVERGENT FORMATION

But ministry leaders have the opportunity through social media to mitigate that individualism through what is known as "social convergence"—a fusion of knowledge, perspectives, experience, and insight across social categories like age, class, economic status, race, denomination, and vocation that have traditionally been separated. Clergy are formed this way, over there, in the seminary. Laypeople are formed that way, in the church. By bringing friends, colleagues, parishioners, organizational members, and skeptics together to respond to a post and to one another's comments, social media facilitates reciprocal learning and invites much broader conceptualizations of key issues of concern to people of faith.

Pastor David Hansen noticed this when he was talking on Facebook with members and colleagues about the death of Osama Bin Laden. He says,

> . . . my non-Christian friends responded to that because it moved them to see a Christian talk about world events in that way, with love and thought. Now, that was not my intended audience, but I think that's one of the ways we reach people who are not in the church, how we talk about our stuff together in ways that they can see. Whether or not you are interacting with those people directly, they are still watching and listening.

Formational convergence happens pretty much all on its own when we engage questions of faith and meaning in social networking communities. But, it can be amplified with a bit more intentionality, as is the case with the dozens upon dozens of large and small covenant groups that gather on Facebook. Ranging from three to nearly a hundred members, these groups are particularly popular for youth ministry, and most are closed so that would-be participants must be granted access by the group administrators. Although we oppose closing general church pages or groups, we think it's a good idea to limit access to social media groups where teens and young adults participate, where personal information may be shared, or where topics discussed might draw hostile outsiders.

Members of the Occupy Boston and Occupy Charleston (SC) protest communities have maintained interreligious Faith and Spirituality Facebook pages where participants share prayers and other spiritual practices for a diversity of traditions, invite one another to worship and other spiritual gatherings, and process the spiritual meanings of the protest movement itself. While not traditional formation by any means, pages like this take

up a formational function, as the wisdom and experience of all participants contribute to collaborative, relationship-based learning. What might it mean for ministry leaders from mainline churches to participate in such spaces, sharing our own social justice traditions and our interreligious values with people we accept and acknowledge as friends on the journey?

Companionship-based learning and formation can also happen in more traditional educational settings. For instance, Darleen Pryds, the church history professor at the Franciscan School of Theology in Berkeley we introduced in Chapter 2, is an advocate for using social media in seminary education and routinely incorporates it into her classes, creating Facebook groups for each class. She recalls one experience that illustrates the way in which learning integrated with social networking extends formation far beyond the event of a particular class or even a semester's worth of study. Says Pryds:

> The class was small—about ten students. Many of us continued to be in touch through Facebook. I've never had a class continue relationships for so long. So, I see them interacting with each other, they interact with me still, and that wouldn't have happened just through email. It just wouldn't have.

For Pryds's students, then, learning is a part of an ongoing relationship among the students and their professor. It changes over time, through regular or even periodic interaction, with learning developing out of participants' shared expertise and insight. However knowledgeable Pryds may be as a spirituality scholar and a medievalist, her real brilliance in this sort of social learning engagement is her ability to facilitate lifelong knowledge-ability among her students.

PREACHING: MAKING PROCLAMATION PARTICIPATORY

Encouraging spiritual knowledge-ability—a collaborative critical reflectiveness on questions of faith and meaning—is of course not limited to the youth group, adult education forum, or seminary classroom. Preaching is also a formational practice that can be opened up and enriched by the social, collaborative, relational ethos of social media communities.

It is not uncommon for those training for ministry in seminaries to come away with the distinct impression that the way to write a good sermon is to withdraw from the world, retreat to the office, and consult Biblical commentaries—oh, and attend to God's guidance. While it is undoubtedly good to incorporate research, critical reflection, prayer, and silence as we attend to the Word and listen for the Holy Spirit, this approach to sermon-writing is very solitary—and, indeed, can be very individualistic. The sermon is essentially the work of one person, and its only connection with the outside world before it's shared from the pulpit is often a scan of the week's news to find connections between the readings and contemporary life.

By contrast, for digital ministers, sermons are the work of many. For many of the same reasons that theological conversations have moved to the local pub, preachers are increasingly writing their sermons in coffee shops. Bill Petersen, the pastor of Faith Lutheran Church in East Hartford, Connecticut, "sermonates" at his local Starbucks, and invites his friends on Facebook to stop by:

> Sermonating @ Starbucks Deming Street, stop on by. My favorite barista gave me grief for not being here for a while . . . she said I must be in need of some good sermon illustrations using the staff (let's hope so).

Here, the sermon is prepared in public and with the public: chatting with the café staff, with people who drop by in person, and with those who link through comments, likes, tweets and retweets in various outposts of the digital community. In this way, preaching, like everything else in social media culture, becomes participatory and collaborative. The sermon is no longer something one person creates and people passively consume. It is something everyone helps to produce. The emphasis shifts from the act of proclamation itself to the conversation leading up to and following it.

This is, of course, entirely consistent with the Latin root of "sermon," *sermo*, which means "discussion." Sister Heather Rollins offers this advice about what we might call a convergent homiletics of transformation in the world of social media:

> It's about conversation. My perspective as a Dominican is that, even for the order of preachers, all the sermons in the world may not convert anybody. But talking and conversing and back and forth and sharing stories—that's what changes hearts.

What is transformative here is not the preacher's words, but the conversation, and the way in which it allows a sermon to speak from the experience of all God's people rather than from the necessarily narrow view of a preacher holed up in her study, noodling over Bible commentaries and grasping for the perfect word. Baptist minister and prolific blogger Tripp Hudgins of First Baptist Church of Palo Alto, California, routinely uses all of his social media networks—Facebook, Twitter, YouTube, and his blog (*anglobaptist.org*)—to develop ideas for upcoming sermons, inspiring both parishioners and clergy colleagues.

Not long ago, for instance, Hudgins (@anglobaptist) posed this question on Twitter: "What is the principle function of the local congregation?" Through the day a wide range of Hudgins's "tweeps"—clergy colleagues, fellow students at the Graduate Theological Union, where Hudgins is currently in the doctoral program, friends from hither and yon—chimed in on the conversation. Part of the exchange went like this:[5]

> **@anglobaptist:** @alanrud @elizabethagan @ABSWBerkeley @JulieCraig @RevJCMitchell @RevMindi What is the function of the local congregation?
>
> **@alanrud:** @anglobaptist @elizabethagan @ABSWBerkeley @JulieCraig @RevJCMitchell @RevMindi To be the hands and feet of Christ.
>
> **@dubpool:** @anglobaptist @alanrud @elizabethagan @ABSWBerkeley @JulieCraig @RevJCMitchell @RevMindi To incarnate Christ in its community?
>
> **@elizabethagan:** @dubpool @anglobaptist @alanrud @ABSWBerkeley @JulieCraig @RevJCMitchell We need community to live out our faith. can't do w/o it

@RevJCMitchell: @dubpool @anglobaptist @alanrud @elizabethagan @ABSWBerkeley @JulieCraig @RevMindi 2B community of liberative & redemptive peeps & witness

@RevJCMitchell: @dubpool @anglobaptist @alanrud @elizabethagan @ABSWBerkeley @JulieCraig @RevMindi As the Body we can live in response to Grace thru Faith

@RevJCMitchell: @RevJCMitchell @dubpool @anglobaptist @alanrud @elizabethagan @ABSWBerkeley @JulieCraig @RevMindi What w/ "local"?

@elizabethagan: @anglobaptist or is the local church really just about people who like to get together and be friends and eat. Sometimes it feels like it.

The extended Twitter conversation fed Hudgins's sermon the following week, carrying the voices of his digital community into the local church. But the conversation went much further, as Hudgins discussed the Twitter conversation in a blog post, which he shared with his Facebook community. This, in turn, allowed his thinking and the wider conversation to influence at least two other sermon writers, who referenced the Twitter exchange Hudgins prompted. In short order, the sermon found its way into a national publication, widening the conversation yet again on his Facebook page and Twitter feed.

Many preachers will tell you that the most successful sermons are the ones inspired by conversation. Whereas a preacher might have only had a few conversations during the week that would influence a sermon, the regular "sermonating" practices of Rollins, Petersen, and Hudgins illustrate that, through social media, preachers can be connected to hundreds of conversations, each filled with new ideas and perspectives that make the Word live in a much richer, relational form. And these are conversations not just with parishioners, but also with colleagues and friends around the world—people who share our faith and those who don't. At times, ministry leaders may initiate the conversation by inviting others to participate with them by posting an idea, an image that's inspired them, or a sentence they've written for an upcoming sermon. They also might post the lectionary readings for the week or pose a question—all with the purpose of eliciting conversation engagement. Thus, the sermon is a collaborative project, not just the musings of a religious "expert."

What's important here is not so much that a better sermon emerges from this networked, relational process—though surely this is the case. What matters is that the process of developing sermons in this collaborative, other-centered way is profoundly formational, engaging a wide array of people in shared reflection on scripture, the life of the church, and its place in the world today. The common practice of spiritual-reflection-in-context that digital ministers like Rollins, Petersen, and Hudgins encourage goes well beyond the sharing of any biblical factoid, however illuminating. It reaches beyond even loving Christian encouragement and inspiration, important though that is. It also models a way of learning that takes its cue not so much from the seminary as from the sanctuary and, more particularly, the communion table, where we all gather to feast on the Word as we prepare to join together as one body.

4.4 BUILDING COMMUNITY: A DIGITAL GLOBAL PARISH

As we've seen, digital social media offer powerful ways to build community. They facilitate increased awareness of each other's lives, providing more occasions for connection and conversation, as well as for the discovery of common interests and passions. The initial social media connection may begin with a designated ministry leader, but the strength of any faith community rests not on relationship to a lay or ordained leader, but on people's relationships to one another and the growth of that trust over time.

At a minimum, ministry leaders and organizations ought to serve as conduits, helping to build community by making digital introductions: tagging people, linking to their work, making friend suggestions, retweeting, and mentioning. This helps members, friends, and colleagues to become aware of one another and sets the stage for friending and following.

Emily Scott, the pastoral minister of St. Lydia's Dinner Church in Brooklyn, New York, which we discussed in Chapter 3, observes how these connections develop on Facebook with people from St. Lydia's:

> I'm always really delighted when I come across a conversation on someone else's Facebook page that's among congregants . . . [I] think, "This is so amazing. These people didn't know each other before they were coming to this church. And these relationships are forming." So, in that way, it's easy for someone to come to the church, meet a few people, to go home and friend them on Facebook and get engaged in that way. . . . It comes before that phase where you're hanging out with each other or it encourages actually hanging out with each other because it's easy to find one another on Facebook.

Many people worry that digital relationships will eclipse face-to-face engagement. However, studies show that people active in social networks are more likely to be engaged in face-to-face volunteerism and faith communities.[6] This is because people who long for community seek it out in many forms, and people who connect in meaningful ways enjoy opportunities to extend that connection in both online and offline settings. Thus, one of the important roles of ministers in social network sites is to cultivate a sense of community that moves between both online and offline locales.

CONNECTING WITH THE LOCAL COMMUNITY

A key ingredient to building a strong community is social capital. Social capital is a term popularized by Robert Putnam in his bestselling book *Bowling Alone: The Collapse and Revival of American Community*, which tracks the alarming weakening of community in America—a trend, it should be noted, that rose primarily out of the separation fostered by broadcast media and which has begun to abate as social media have developed.[7] Social capital can be defined as "the collective value of all 'social networks' [who people know] and the inclinations that arise from these networks to do things for each other."[8]

David Crowley is working to strengthen social capital in several Massachusetts communities, including his home town of Woburn, through the non-profit organization he founded, Social Capital, Inc. The organization has programs that promote youth leadership, volunteerism, and civic engagement. Crowley himself is an avid user of social media and sees a role for it to play in the work of building community:

> At the end of the day, our goal is to get people more engaged and connected, and we have to think about where people are. [C]larifying the role that technology plays for us—that it's a means to an end—actually pushed us to say it's not just about our website, it's about using whatever means are out there that make sense to achieve our goals.

Crowley (@DC_Woburn) models this in his own social media practice. He personally checks in around his home community on Foursquare, highlighting local institutions and activities like the children's library program and the farmers' market. He identifies local people on Facebook and Twitter and interacts with them regularly. He is deliberate, purposeful, and consistent, using digital and face-to-face connections to reinforce one another and strengthen community connections.

Crowley particularly likes Twitter for its ability to create entirely new connections and build relationships within a local community:

> The openness of the platform was pretty exciting and consistent with our mission. . . . Part of our approach is to have the community be a welcoming place for anybody, whether you've been here for three generations or three days. . . . But the reality is that it doesn't often happen that way. I think [Twitter] does have this way of opening up and inviting . . . You can engage even if you don't have an existing relationship with me.

He continues, highlighting the way in which Twitter conversations create opportunities for face-to-face connection:

> What I like about using social media in a local setting is that we might start chatting on Twitter about eating local foods but then there's a potential, if there is real shared interest there, to go and do something offline, create a more substantial relationship.

As we'll discuss more in what follows, we see this "something offline" invited by online engagement as the incarnational potential of social media participation.

BRIDGING AND BONDING SOCIAL CAPITAL

It is worth noting, too, that Crowley makes sure to model the kind of mutually engaging community his organization promotes by practicing reciprocity within his local Twitter community, following back everyone who follows him. This creates a clear message that he's about genuine, balanced community rather than about blasting out messages that highlight his perspectives over the insights of others. This develops social—and spiritual—capital in two particular ways—bridging and bonding.[9] *Bridging capital* creates connections between people who don't already know one another, helping people discover common points of intersection, creating new relationships and links. *Bonding capital* strengthens the ties between people with existing relationships. Twitter is particularly good for building bridging social capital, while Facebook is good for building bonding social capital. Developing either, however, depends on exercising reciprocity in how you engage with others.

A HOLY NETWORK

For blogger Adam Copeland (*adamcopeland.com*), social media is central to creating and sustaining community, and he sees different relationships developing on different platforms and in different ways. Copeland, a Presbyterian minister, is a bit of a mash-up himself. His mission developer for a Lutheran young adult ministry in the university town of Fargo, North Dakota. Copeland's challenge from the Evangelical Lutheran Church in America has been to create community among the forty-five thousand young adults in the Fargo-Moorhead area who are not connected to a church. "Obviously," says

Copeland, "what we're doing in the church just isn't connecting for young adults." This motivated the ELCA's leaders to take more of a community organizing approach to engage.

The resulting mission, "Project F-M" (Fargo-Moorhead), is focused on engaging eighteen-to-twenty-five-year-olds by listening to their stories and attending to how questions of faith and meaning play out in their lives. Copeland has initiated a number of innovative occasions for connecting— theology pubs, a "WTF" (Where's the Faith) study group, and "Holy City" worship events at parks, train depots, and other locations around the city. But these connections depend heavily on social media.

"Social media is the primary way I connect with young adults," says Copeland. "Our Facebook group has grown a good deal in the past few months, and that's mostly where I interact with people who might be interested in what we're doing. I interact with people much more on Facebook than on the website."

Copeland shares information on upcoming events with the more than three hundred members of the group page, but he goes well beyond using the page simply as a digital bulletin board. "I write messages to anyone who's come to an event who's on Facebook," Copeland explains. "I want people to know we saw they were there, we know their name. And then I let them know about what might be coming up, and give them a link to a Google map to the event."

Copeland tries to encourage day-to-day interactivity among participants on the page by, for instance, posting short notes about what people talked about at the most recent theology pub and asking follow-up questions. "I want to invite people to reflect," he says, and that invitation might result in people sharing links to more information on the topic, comments, or, in one recent case, a Robert Louis Stevenson poem from one of the folks who attended a theology pub on how God speaks to us today.

All of this digital engagement reinforces the face-to-face engagement and, not unimportantly, extends it across the networks of all the participants. Says Copeland of how this supports his ministry and how different social media platforms come into play in his ministry:

> Because I am as active as I am in social media, I have a pretty wide view of the community, and I know a lot of what's going on that I really wouldn't otherwise know. . . . I use Facebook to be a friendly figure from the church, to be connected to different communities, and to share resources. . . .
>
> I use Twitter to make connections more, most often locally. And I ask questions on Twitter or share short comments that don't really rise to a Facebook post.
>
> The blog is really my filter . . . it's where I'm thinking through things, and mostly that engages colleagues in ministry. It's a way for me to reflect, to explore different ideas, and it functions as a kind of check within a community. It keeps me aware that I'm not in ministry alone.

This integrated, multiplatform social media participation gives digital ministers like Copeland the opportunity to develop and nurture a variety of communities among those he serves as well as his colleagues, supporting his ministry and helping it to grow. Such practices are especially important for connecting with people who, for whatever reason, have not felt invited into our communities or who feel alienated from them. Says another young adult minister, Alicia Saunders, a campus minister at a Roman Catholic high school in California's Central Valley, "If I weren't on Facebook, my students would hardly know I existed. I'd just be 'that chick who makes everyone go to chapel.' It's ironic, maybe, but by being who I am on Facebook—just really myself, not all Ms. Religion—I'm more real to the teenagers I serve."

A HUMBLE WALK

Pastor Jodi Bjornstad Houge is building community and making faith connections in the West End neighborhood of St. Paul, Minnesota, where she founded Humble Walk Lutheran Church, a mission start of the ELCA. It began with a vision of a Christian congregation deeply embedded in the life and rhythm of the West End neighborhood. Bjornstad Houge explains,

> We recognized that most people don't come looking for a church, in our demographic. And so, we thought from the beginning, "We know this. The church is sinking." The facts are on the table for the mainline denominations. So, we're not going to do these big glossy things that try and draw people to our cool, fancy, hip church. We're going to be where people already are and try to be the church where they are.

Humble Walk doesn't have a church building and has no desire for one. Their first worship services were held in a coffee shop, and since then they have worshipped in a storefront, a public park, and an art gallery. Humble Walk intentionally has all of its gatherings in public spaces within the West End in order to worship, learn, and serve "where people are."

This is parish ministry in its broadest sense, where the borders and walls between insiders and outsiders, church and community, are blurred and even erased. One of those public places is Facebook, where Humble Walk hosts an active group page.

The Facebook group is Humble Walk's central meeting place as well as its main form of communication. In addition to weekly "enouncements" and updates, there are also moments of random fun and inspiration, and expressions of care and gratitude. Facebook keeps the congregation connected and helps them connect to the community. Indeed, Facebook helps Humble Walk to fulfill its mission of embedded, decentralized ministry because it serves as the congregation's central hub.

As with the Project F-M ministry Copeland leads, Humble Walk's social media participation has everything to do with nurturing local community

and face-to-face relationship, developing the social capital that will carry the faith to successive generations and to people who have often been excluded from mainline churches. When we recall, as we discussed in Chapter 2, that Facebook and Twitter are particularly active sites of engagement for people under age thirty and, especially on Twitter, for people of color, we see the significance of extending our ministries into digital communities by way of strengthening, rather than competing with or replacing, local communities.

4.5 MAKING PUBLIC WITNESS

At the heart of building community—and every art of ministry, digital or otherwise—is the love of neighbor. Making public witness is about making that love visible in online and offline environments. This may include food and clothing collection for needy neighbors, helping to build a home with Habitat for Humanity, advocating on particular issues, or standing with neighbors in challenging times. Today it also includes using social media platforms to raise awareness, rally people to a cause, and call them to action.

Social media have vastly expanded the ability to communicate, publicize, coordinate, and share this work. In *Here Comes Everybody: The Power of Organizing Without Organizing*, Clay Shirky writes, "The current change, in one sentence, is this: most of the barriers to group action have collapsed, and without those barriers, we are free to explore new ways of gathering together and getting things done."[10] We have seen this in powerful ways in the 2011 Arab Spring, and Occupy Wall Street, which Douglas Rushkoff has called, "America's first true internet-era movement."[11] Church leaders and organizations are just beginning to leverage the power of social media for advocating and acting for social justice.

CALLING ALL CROWS

Matt Wilhelm is among those at the forefront of using social media for social justice. Wilhelm is the co-executive director of Calling All Crows, a Boston-based non-profit organization that advocates for the empowerment of women around the world through issue advocacy, hands-on volunteerism, and humanitarian aid. They have raised over $200,000 for women in Sudan and Afghanistan, and have coordinated ten thousand hours of service in local communities.

Calling All Crows was founded by Chad Stokes, of the bands Dispatch and State Radio, and band manager Sybil Gallagher. The "indie rock star" effect gives Calling All

Crows a distinct advantage in terms of garnering attention, and the organization orients its engagement toward musicians and their fans in particular. The challenge, however, is getting people who are interested in music to be interested and passionate about social justice. Through Facebook, Twitter, and the *Crows' Nest* blog on their website, Calling All Crows helps fans become knowledgeable about women's justice issues, to connect with others who are concerned about the well-being of women, and to take action to support women's empowerment. In this, Wilhelm says, the group rounds out traditional broadcast messaging approaches with more interactive social engagement aimed at developing relationships:

> You bring people in—they either sign up on your mailing list, follow you on Twitter, or find us on Facebook—and then it's about pushing out some messages that are supporting a particular campaign that we're a part of. The next step is to engage them somehow. . . . Say, we're asking a question, we receive a response, and we acknowledge them. And taking the next step . . . reaching out to them in some way, saying, 'Hey, what's going on, I noticed that you did this, that, or the other thing. Have you signed up for . . . ?" That direct engagement shows that this is more than a mouthpiece, more than just a message being broadcast. . . . It's not about the social media or the email, it's about how we develop a relationship. That's what makes people think: relationship. . . . This isn't just about social media, it's about real relationships with people.

It is these personal engagements with the organization's staff members, who are themselves active on social media, that cultivate the conversations and connections that can lead to working for justice together. These personal and organizational platforms are the entry points for engaging, educating, and taking action in one of Calling All Crows' social justice campaigns.

Kim Warick, a communications intern at Calling All Crows, highlights the important link between what happens on the Facebook page or Twitter feed and incarnational, face-to-face participation that changes the lives of women across the globe:

> The whole conversation isn't going on in social media. We're trying to get people engaged there and then direct them to the meat of what we do, which is in other places. . . . We try to make it conversational and not super heavy. You only have a certain number of characters to work with, so keeping it short and quick and, if it catches people's interests, then giving the resource to go and find out more about it."

Social media serve as the entry point for campaigns like "Bringing Change to Women," which raises funds for the building of safe shelters for women in Afghanistan, and a domestic maternal health initiative. In addition, every time Stokes plays a concert, there is also a volunteer service opportunity. Calling All Crows uses social media to publicize, coordinate, and share that work.

CALLING ALL CHURCHES

The work of Calling All Crows is instructive for ministry leaders and congregations. The focus on engagement, the availability of the staff, action born out of relationships—all of these things mark what we see as the fully incarnational potential of social networking. As Shirky writes, "Our social tools are turning love into a renewable building material. When people care enough, they can come together and accomplish things of a scope and longevity that were previously impossible; they can do big things for love."[12] Certainly, if our churches can't grasp the significance of this kind of engagement, we give up any hope of having relevance or engaging meaningfully in the lives of people today and in the generations to come.

4.6 Extended Profile: Nadia Bolz-Weber, Sarcastic Lutheran

Nadia Bolz-Weber is the founding pastor of House for All Sinners and Saints (HFASS), an emerging church Lutheran mission started in Denver, Colorado. Bolz-Weber is recognized among her peers as one of the most unmistakable voices in the church. She is active on Twitter and Facebook, and maintains a popular sermon blog and personal website, which pulls together these social media.

Bolz-Weber's entry into social media began with blogging when she was a student at Pacific Lutheran Theological Seminary in Berkeley, California. "I just needed an outlet. Some people encouraged me to do it. They said, 'You should have a blog. You're always spouting off at the mouth. So, you should really do it that way.' . . . I was encouraged by others. I had an external call to blogging."

"With Facebook, it was personal and then eventually it became a way to get the word out there. I didn't intend to be a public figure on Facebook, it's just the more speaking I did, the more people were friending me who I didn't know. Once again, there was a sort of external call. People would say, 'Thanks for posting that,' or, 'We're going to use that,' or, 'I appreciated your sermon.'"

"It all happened without it being a contrivance, without it being a technique or plan or strategy of any kind," Bolz-Weber explains. "Also, people in my environment, in my cultural context, are pretty tech savvy. They're native to this stuff, so it's just natural."

One of the reasons Bolz-Weber is so effective is that she has a clear and consistent voice—the same voice you hear whether you talk to her in person, text her, or tweet back and forth. It is also well defined. You can find it on her Twitter handle and blog title, "Sarcastic Lutheran"—a name she can't remember how she came up with, but which seems to everyone who encounters her to fit. She is, indeed, "sarcastic" in a way that both loves and critiques the church. She runs from anything that reeks of an overwrought theology or which has the taint of church marketing. For instance, Bolz-Weber may invite people to worship by quipping, "It doesn't suck."

Describing her voice, Bolz-Weber says:

> Honest to God, I'm just me. I just am lucky enough to have work in which I can totally be who I am. I'm just lucky to have a job where I can have a consistent voice, and that voice is actually mine. I have a lot of colleagues for whom that's not true. They have to really manage their own personalities to a large extent in their work, and I don't.
>
> Since I don't, I think that's really inviting to other people. They get it when they're around me or read something I write. They know that it's just a real person, a whole person, who is flawed and faithful at the same time and who's inviting for them in a way that more manicured personalities aren't going to be

as inviting. I try to keep it real as much as I can, and sometimes that gets me in trouble, but sometimes it's a really transformative thing for myself and others.

While Bolz-Weber doesn't claim a neatly coordinated digital ministry strategy, she does follow what we might call digital spiritual practices that invite engagement in her local and distributed communities, provide inspiration and encouragement, and connect digital disciples to those in the House for All Sinners and Saints community:

> Before morning prayer I'll often throw up a tweet that says, "Text or Facebook or tweet your [prayer] requests," and people do. We, literally, on Wednesday mornings, are praying for a bunch of people we don't even know. But it's like this promise we are sending out: We promise that if you send us something—it doesn't matter who you are, or what connection you have or don't have to the community—we'll pray for you. And that connects us to all kinds of people.

Like other particularly effective digital ministers, Bolz-Weber uses social media to make sermon preparation a communal practice with both formational value and sacramental echoes. For instance, when preparing a sermon, she asked her Facebook friends what came to mind when they heard John 3:16—"For God so loved the world that he gave his only Son, that everyone who believes in him may not perish but have eternal life." She received forty-seven responses, and what the majority of people pictured was Rollen Stewart, a born-again Christian fixture at sporting events who wears a rainbow wig and holds up signs that say "John 3:16," with a matching t-shirt (or a coordinating one that reads "Jesus Saves" on the front and "Repent" on the back) to help bring the point home. Stewart's whacky rainbow wig and stadium proselytizing was the launch point for Bolz-Weber's sermon.[13]

Unlike other preachers we admire who use social networking to develop sermons collaboratively, Bolz-Weber's focus here was more about the basics of social media participation that we discussed at the beginning of the chapter: listening, attending, connecting, and engaging. We certainly recommend that you surf over to the full sermon, but we won't rehearse it all here. What we highlight as a best practice in digital ministry, though, is the sustained attentiveness that Bolz-Weber paid to what Rollen Stewart (and what many of us see as manipulative or even abusive uses of John 3:16) meant to members of her community. Her sermon spoke to their frustration and to the offense that misguided uses of scripture cause to those truly intent on sharing God's love with all people—sinners and saints alike. Bolz-Weber preached specifically to the concerns of her community, echoing what she heard as their concern that "the best way to exclude someone else is to make the entire God-loving-the-world thing not about God's extravagant Love, but about our belief." This is the fruit of deep, prophetic listening, as is the reassurance she offers at the end of the sermon:

> God has swept you up into God's redemptive love for the whole world and there is nothing for you to add: no amount of belief, no giving up of sweets during Lent, no good works. Nothing.

Now, clearly, Bolz-Weber is a gifted theological thinker and an inspiring writer. We need not doubt that she would have come up with an awesome sermon without such engagement. But it would have been *her* sermon, *her* insights, *her* reflections. And while surely those, too, would have been lovely and encouraging, what her Facebook conversation permitted was the crafting of a sermon that spoke from and for and to the people she serves. Such prophetic homiletics doesn't require social media, but social media does open the pastor's study to lots more voices.

And to that, the people generally say, "Amen."

4.7 EXTENDED PROFILE: *FATHER MATTHEW PRESENTS*

Father Matthew Moretz, Associate Rector of St. Bartholomew Episcopal Church in New York, New York, describes YouTube as "an inculturating tool that's actually fun." He is the originator of the series *Father Matthew Presents*, light-hearted video vignettes on issues of faith and ministry. "The treasures of Christianity, one video at a time," says Moretz.

Moretz has been YouTubing since 2006, and his videos have been viewed over half a million times. Today *Father Matthew Presents* is a well-known and very well-produced series, but it began simply when Father Matthew, in an effort to revive the church he was serving at the time, started a video blog on YouTube.

In the early videos, he is sitting in his office. A blackboard behind him showed the date and the title of the video. One of our favorites is the one of Moretz playing the *Super Mario Bros.* theme song on the church carillon. Such videos garnered attention and sparked conversation within and well beyond the Episcopal Church.

If Moretz's approach evokes memories of *Mr. Rogers' Neighborhood*, that's by design. "I want people to have a relationship with a priest just like I had a relationship with Mr. Rogers. And that relationship with Mr. Rogers is forever for me. He formed my soul."

He continues:

> Here's the thing: nobody cares about just a priest talking. Nobody. You have to have something else. That's the problem with the sermon. You've got to add something to it. It has to be entertaining. There has to be a twist to it.
>
> . . . A priest on a screen, not just talking, but a priest in a sequential moving-image play, allows for more occasions to identify with the church, to be formed by the church, to give people room in their hearts for the Gospel, because they have a relationship with someone through a screen.

Moretz creates video magic with a reasonably priced HD camera, a green screen, three lights, and video editing software. He posts one video a month that takes about nine hours from start to finish, including writing the scripts.

Moretz advises:

> It's good to start with something simple. What I've learned is: I don't believe in three-point sermons. One point. You've got to get one point across, because people's attention spans are going down the tubes. What people retain from a sermon is so minimal . . .
>
> People are able to critically analyze video and TV and film like scholars, but if you show them a book or a sermon, their critical faculties are poor. But with a movie or TV, they can pick it apart. They have all kinds of critical tools to deal with it, to chew on it, digest it. They have the enzymes for it- because they were raised on it day in and day out, but they weren't raised on sermons or books. What I try to do is read the books that matter, listen to the sermons that matter, and translate the good stuff into video.

Moretz attributes much of his success with the *Father Matthew Presents* series to his attention to how other filmmakers ply their craft—professional and amateur alike. Here's more advice on how to start a video ministry project:

- Before you launch your video ministry, take a look at top view-getters in the religion community on YouTube. For example, check out the over-the-top religious commentary of Betty Butterfield.
- Pay attention to how shots are set up, scenes constructed, and narratives rolled out in your favorite TV shows. How would you give your church a reality-show feel? What would live reporting from your latest community service project look like? How would Stephen Colbert talk about social justice? And, let's not forget puppets.

What Moretz's YouTube ministry success illustrates is that you don't have to present with talking heads and dry sermonating. Take creative risks. In social media, they often pay off.

4.8 EXTENDED PROFILE: MASSACHUSETTS COUNCIL OF CHURCHES

The Massachusetts Council of Churches, an ecumenical organization whose mission is to help churches to work together to "express Christian unity as fully and visibly as possible," faced the same sort of challenges all churches see in a time of incredible cultural change—only multiplied by 1,700.

The 1,700 or so member churches supported by the council depend in particular on executive director Laura Everett and her small staff for access to information about what's going on in the statewide faith community that they wouldn't get through denominational channels. And, because the mission of the organization highlights expressing unity "through joint planning, mutual counsel, and common programming," it's important that they have that information in a timely manner and in a form that highlights how neighboring churches can participate in key initiatives and events.

"Historically we've thought about the Mass Council of Churches as being a kind of hub and the denominations are spokes," says Everett, "so information comes in and goes back out and it was up to the staff and the board to be a conduit for that information." In a way, the organization was

a pre-internet information aggregator, passing along news from the Presbyterian church in Lowell to the Methodist church in Tewksbury, if it seemed like there might be a common interest.

Through a strategic planning process that highlighted communications, Everett explains, the council "clearly acknowledged that the communications networks that we were previously using just weren't viable. . . . In the time that I've been there, most of [the member denominations] have stopped printing paper newsletters. In the last seven years, it's become clear that the lag time was increasing with every year."

But, new ways of communicating and the need for faster information sharing was not the whole of the problem. Through the early 2000s, says Everett, "the nature of a council of churches was changing. . . . As denominational structures have changed, that is not necessarily the only place in which we want to think about ecumenism happening, or our only partners. Our communication strategy needed to match what our organization was."

As with many churches, individual ministry leaders, and other religious organizations, the council considers Facebook to be central to a more networked communication approach. "That's where most of our people are right now," says Everett, so the sharing of information moved from emails and faxes to posts on the group's Facebook wall. Here, the significance of communicating within a network, rather than as the hub broadcasting to isolated spokes, immediately became clear. Says Everett, "It turned out it hasn't been that big a shift because I was always forwarding those emails anyway. But the ripple effect is bigger now that I can take that email I would have sent . . . and put it up online and tag you in it."

This connects the story on the council's Facebook page to the networks of everyone who has liked the page, vastly expanding the organization's reach, but, more than that, expanding the diversity of people whom they are engaging. This more widely networked engagement depends, of course, on developing relationships in meaningful ways. Everett and the council staff approach nurturing connections in two ways—the first having to do with content, the second with reciprocity.

Because members are already networked themselves, passing around news that everyone is getting through denominational channels—and increasingly across them—is hardly a value-added service. So, Everett focuses on enriching the content she shares. "I try to make sure to have a little something you wouldn't know from the *Globe* article I linked to—something I know about the people that are in play or the relationships we've built," she explains. "I always want to be communicating beyond a posed photo."

Everett describes the work they do on behalf of members as being like "a curator" of information and connections. She asks questions about the information she comes across as she considers what it means for members. Everett explains her editorial approach to sharing information of interest to member churches:

> If I come across stories on human trafficking, gambling, immigration, the environment, poverty, I'm always asking, "What does this tell about my organization? What am I supposed to glean from this relative to your organization? How can I link things together that haven't been put together to add value to the content, to tell a larger story?" . . . I have a goal for myself of getting something up three to five times a day, during the work day. I wanted it to be related to Massachusetts, related to ecumenism, or to one of the denominations, to one of our member churches that others might not hear about.

Getting out even enriched content to a more diverse matrix of networks isn't the whole of the social media strategy used by the Massachusetts Council of Churches. Building relationships is critical, and that requires close listening and attentiveness to what members are doing and sharing in their social media spaces. Everett takes particular care to share the accomplishments of member churches and to acknowledge the contributions of others, an act of digital graciousness that goes a long way toward deepening connections:

> I go to the Facebook news feed and "like" a ton of stuff and thank people—especially when I use something from a denomination or one of our local churches, even to share it. I make sure to give credit and praise people for good ministry. One of the best things about my job is that I get to see some really great ministry in a ton of places. It used to be that, as the hub, we were the only ones who had access to that privileged information.

These relationships have helped the council to make connections within congregations that would not have been possible in the Broadcast Age. "When I started all this I was thinking about how we get our message out," says Everett. "But what it's allowed me to do more of is see what I need to respond to. One of the things social media has been really good for is helping us connect with individual congregations and individual people who are passionate about ecumenism."

This networked, relational digital ministry requires, according to Everett, "integrity across platforms" and a balancing of voices that she navigates across the organizational page and her own Facebook page. Her sensitivity to the role of a leader within an organization with a longer ministry horizon is particularly instructive. Everett makes sure to post first on the council Facebook page and then to share on her own wall. She explains:

> Sometimes it seems like people like the personal voice better, but it's the Mass Council of Churches. It's not the Council of Laura. I don't ever want to be in a position where nobody else can do the work afterwards because I've so become aligned with the organization that there's no other imaginative possibility.

In the end, Everett is convinced that engaging in social media communities is critical for shaping a positive, productive conversation about Christian unity:

> If we're not there, we're conceding space. Somebody else will take it. And if I'm not helping to craft a conversation, an intelligent conversation, about Christian unity, it will happen somewhere else, but it will happen without me. I can't presume the authority, but media can cultivate it by creating a good space and having good content and asking thoughtful questions and giving thanks for the good ways that people do manifest that unity.

DIGITAL MINISTRY STRATEGY: THE ARTS OF DIGITAL MINISTRY

The following questions are designed to help you reflect on how you are practicing the arts of digital ministry. Reflect on them for you personally and, either on your own or with a group, in the context of your ministry community.

1. Using the LACE framework for digital ministry, reflect on the ways you currently—or may in the future—listen, attend, connect, and engage in social networking.

   Listening—taking time to get to know people in social networks rather than shouting your message

   _____

   _____

   _____

   Attending—being present to the experiences and interest of others

   _____

   _____

   _____

   Connecting—reaching out to others in diverse communities in order to deepen and extend networks

   _____

   _____

   _____

Engaging—building relationships by sharing content, collaborating, connecting people to others

_____

_____

_____

2. Using the categories we described for the arts of digital ministry, note where you see yourself as most comfortable now and what might be a growth area for you. How might you develop in your growth areas? You might want to complete this assessment for both yourself and for your church or organization.

	Comfort Zone?	Growth Area?	How?
Offering Hospitality	❑	❑	_____
Caring for God's People	❑	❑	_____
Forming Disciples	❑	❑	_____
Building Community	❑	❑	_____
Making Public Witness	❑	❑	_____

CONCLUSION
Digital Incarnation

 In most relationships that begin in digital locales, the reality of authentic, personal, mutual relationship invites a face-to-face connection. This desire for incarnation, as we churchy types might call it, is the real beauty and power of digital ministry.

WE FINISHED WRITING AND EDITING the bulk of *Click 2 Save* just as the snow was starting to fly in Boston, Keith's hometown, and winter rains began to fall in San Jose, where Elizabeth lives. But, when we met face-to-face for the first time it was nothing like that. For a few days in the late fall, Keith left behind what turned out to be the first snow of the season to wing his way into a gloriously beautiful Northern California weekend. Our Facebook walls and Foursquare profiles blossomed with photos of the Monterey coast drenched with sun, the Carmel Lone Cypress just before sunset, San Francisco's Grace Cathedral reaching up to a deep blue, cloudless sky on the warm Sunday when we had the opportunity to hear our editor, Stephanie Spellers,[1] preach about how the church can change—must change—if we have any intention of continuing to do God's work in a world in which "the way we've always done it" simply doesn't resonate with most people.

According to researchers at the Pew Forum on Religion & Public Life, about thirty percent of people who were raised as Roman Catholics will leave the church as adults, half of those affiliating with another religious tradition, half with none at all. Bleak though that may sound, for mainline Protestants, the picture is even bleaker. More than fifty percent of people raised in Methodist, Lutheran, Presbyterian, Episcopalian, and Congregationalist churches will leave as adults, about a third of those claiming no identification with institutional churches.[2] And, as most of us involved in churches probably know from our own observation and experience, the drain among the fifty-and-under crowd is significantly greater—which kind of makes both of us church-going, spiritual freaks.

Clearly, we have to do something different if we're going to continue to connect with believers and seekers and engage them in the very real work of creating God's kingdom on earth. And, yet, at the end of the day, it is just as clear that we cannot simply click to save—to save the church, to save souls (whatever that might mean in these postmodern, post-Christian times), to save the world. Though this may mean that we've led you down something of a digital primrose path, it's clear to us that participation in social networking communities is not the answer.

That is, at least not on its own. Not as a tool, or a gimmick. Not as an add-on to "real" ministry practice.

DIGITAL MINISTRY IS NOT DIGITAL MARKETING

Throughout this book, we've echoed, quite deliberately, two key themes that bear repeating one more time as we come to the end of this particular part of our pilgrimage together. The first is that digital ministry is not the same as digital marketing. Very much at the center of the challenges facing the church is the challenge of communicating what the Gospel means—how it invites us to live in the light of God's grace in relation to one another and creation—with new generations of seekers and believers. But communicating is sharing language, ideas, stories, images and so on with others, in community, in service of the common good. That is, in relationships of mutual respect and caring. In communion.

Marketing, on the other hand, is about relating transactionally to others—not *being in relationship with*, but *relating to* others—by way, according to the folks at Merriam-Webster, "of promoting and selling products and services." For whatever it might do in the service of another, it wants something back. It wants you to buy, join, pledge, pay.

That doesn't mean that all marketing is inherently evil or even just plain bad. We have lots of respect for people who tell the stories of their products and services with integrity and creativity. And we admire those who understand the importance of respectful, long-term relationships with customers. Still, we have assumed throughout *Click 2 Save* that marketing is not the way of Christ, and it's not the purpose of digital ministry. As Elizabeth insisted in *Tweet If You* ♥ *Jesus*, "It's not that 'church marketing sucks,' as much as it is that marketing the church sucks."[3] It's just not how we think ministry is meant to play out in the Christian tradition.

DIGITAL MINISTRY IS RELATIONAL AND NETWORKED

This assumption leads directly to the second theme that we've nailed to the doorposts throughout the book: digital ministry is relational and networked, and these relational networks reach far beyond the local church.

Now, as it happens, we think this is true of all ministry. We take our cue on this from Jesus' instructions to his most immediate disciples, who were called not to establish churches *per se*, but to journey throughout the nations (Matt. 10:1–19; Matt. 28:16–20), to share God's healing love among God's people (e.g., Matt. 8:14-17, 9:18-32; Mark 2:1-12, 9:14-29; John 5:1-9), and to proclaim God's kingdom (Luke 9:1–3) not as some futuristic fantasy, but as real and present in the love and compassion of one human being in relation to another. "They departed and went through the villages, bringing the good news and curing diseases everywhere," Luke's gospel tells us (Luke 9:6). Christianity, it turns out, is a road trip, not a building. It is, that is, relational and networked. And, certainly, it is mobile.

DIGITAL MINISTRY IS INCARNATIONAL

All of which bring us to perhaps the most important theme, one which came into sharp relief for us on that autumn weekend when we first met face-to-face, we two writers and our editor, along with the artist who created most of the images in the book. We had gathered to weave together the final threads of the story we offer in *Click 2 Save*—a story about how relational, networked ministry in digital spaces and in local churches and religious organizations is the best hope for making the church relevant and engaged in everyday life again.

Fully two-thirds of American adults are active in social networking communities. Nearly 100 percent of teens are actively online and 80 percent regularly use social networking sites. The bulk of both teens and adults use their digital participation as a vital and vibrant part of their relationships with friends and families.[4] Digital engagement is now the reality of human experience in America and in most of the world.

What's more, the available data tell us over and over again that digital media are profoundly incarnational. They do what broadcast media could

Keith on pilgrimage in Cupertino, CA

never do: connect us more deeply to those we know already, and extend real and meaningful relationship to those we may know only indirectly—only as links in the helixed DNA of the Body of Christ. But for the two of us, as our digital relationship developed while Elizabeth was researching and writing *Tweet If You ♥ Jesus* and blossomed into a genuine friendship through the writing of this book, the data we mined as we worked on *Click 2 Save* was mere confirmation of what we knew in our actual, physical bones: digital media had connected us spiritually, and the truth of that connection had a deep incarnational pull. Our weekly Google+ video hangouts made us want to hang out in person, to break bread and to tramp common ground together.

So it was that our time together that late October weekend played out as the incarnate end of a digitally integrated pilgrimage, the penultimate stop of which was on the ground where the technology that allowed us to connect was, in some fashion at least, created: the Apple headquarters in Cupertino, CA. There, not long after the death of Apple founder Steve Jobs, people from around the world had come to walk the Apple campus, to make real in their bodies the space from which a remarkable spirit of creativity, collaboration, and beauty had contributed so much to individuals, relationships, and communities. We paid homage with the rest.

But that, of course, was not the whole of it. Our time together was populated with other friends and other conversations, our network expanding in relational depth even as we completed the last phases of the book.

Perhaps not surprisingly, this part of our pilgrimage closed in worship, our friendship tied to a faith that is at the core of our commitment to practices of ministry centered on listening to others, attending to the needs of the world the church serves, connecting across diverse and widely distributed networks, and engaging believers and seekers wherever they may be. This, notwithstanding our periodic frustrations with what can seem like the church's intractable inability to engage the world as it is *now* and our eagerness to contribute to new ways of being the Body of Christ in the world. Our worship, then, was something of a prayer of gratitude for the opportunity to work together on this project and a petition for a more widely networked community of ministry leaders who are eager to try new approaches to church, new ways of animating the Body of Christ in the digitally integrated world.

We pray that you are among those leaders. We hope you will join us in this pilgrimage, connecting your digital ministry to those of others who see Facebook, Twitter, YouTube, and other social networking communities as real and significant sites for practices of mission and ministry that are as transformative as they are incarnational. We hope you will invite disenchanted and disengaged believers and seekers into relationships that move easily from digital spaces to local ones, and back again. We know our friendship and faith have benefited from the journey, and we know your participation on the road ahead will only bring more of the blessings we have shared to more people and communities across the world. We hope that together we can all click—and connect and invite and engage and tell our stories of faith and its implications far and wide—and thus help revitalize the church we love. The church that has saved us both.

GLOSSARY

Term	Definition	Page
aggregator	Application which pulls together web content in one place, such as Google Reader for blogs. A person or organization can also function as an aggregator by consistently sharing information in a particular area of interest (e.g., *Huffington Post* is a news aggregator).	85
Bing	A search engine created by Microsoft to compete with Google. The Bing search engine powers searches on the popular sites Yahoo and Facebook.	179
blog	Derived from a mash-up of the words "web" and "log," blogs are platforms for sharing written content but also video (sometimes called "vlogs," or video logs) and photos. *http://word press.com, http://blogger.com, http://typepad.com, http://tumbler.com, http://posterous.com*	4
bridging capital	Social capital developed through making connections between people who don't already know one another, helping people discover points of intersection, creating new relationships and links. [See also "social capital."]	154
bonding capital	Social capital developed through strengthening the ties between people with existing relationships. [See also "social capital."]	154
check-in	A social media check-in lets people in your network know where you are located at any given moment.	53
connection	A person in a LinkedIn member's professional network.	88

Term	Definition	Page
cloud	Cloud computing is provided by companies who offer software, data access, and data storage services to users remotely, from computer servers in locations unknown to users—or, in the clouds. Such services allow users to reduce storage on their own computers and devices and allow them to access their files wherever they are in the world.	180
crowdsourcing	The gathering of globally distributed participants in loosely organized communities for the purpose of collaborating to solve a problem or advocate for change.	19
digital ministry	The set of practices that extend spiritual care, formation, prayer, evangelism, and other manifestations of grace into online spaces like Facebook, Twitter, and YouTube, where more and more people gather to nurture, explore, and share their faith today.	1
Digital Reformation	A revitalization of the church driven largely by the *ad hoc* spiritualities of ordinary believers influenced by digital social networking.	7
Dropbox	Cloud-based file sharing application, which syncs documents between devices and the web. [See also "cloud."] *http://dropbox.com*	10
Facebook	The world's largest digital social network. *http://facebook.com*	1
Flickr	A photo hosting and sharing website that functions as a digital photo album. *http://flickr.com*	55
follow/ followers	People who join your network on Twitter "follow" you. They are then referred to as your "followers."	25
Follow Friday (#FF)	On Fridays, many Twitter users recommend other users they find particularly interesting, valuable, or fun to follow.	79

Term	Definition	Page
Foursquare	Geo-location social media platform that works with global positioning systems (GPS) on smart phones to let people in your network know your location through checking in. *http://foursquare.com*	6
friending/ friend	The practice of inviting people into your network on Facebook. People who accept friend requests are "friends" in your Facebook network regardless of their personal relationship.	33
Google	The world's largest online search engine. Google also offers email (Gmail), advertising services, and a wide range of other online services, including the Google+ social networking site. *http://google.com*	17
Google+	Social network created by Google. Similar in functionality to Facebook, it organizes connections into circles and includes video chatting with up to 10 people at once. *http://google.com*	3
hashtag	Twitter's version of tags, marked with a # symbol to designate an area of interest, topic, or community. [See also "tags."]	35
Kiva	An online micro-lending service that enables donors to give small amounts for projects created by people and organizations in underserved communities. *http://kiva.com*	20
LinkedIn	The largest social network for business professionals. *http://linkedin.com*	3
meme	From the Greek *mimeme*, meaning "something imitated or copied," a meme in social networking is a catchphrase, idea, story, or practice that is replicated across a social network (e.g., "nomnom" is a meme for chewing food based on a popular video of a cat eating).	181
mention	When someone's Twitter username is included in a tweet. This can be part of a public conversation or a shout-out.	35

Term	Definition	Page
MicroPlace	A micro-investment service that enables people to invest in projects around the world that address social problems. *https://www.microplace.com*	20
MySpace	One of the first social networking sites, largely used by pre-teens, teens, and bands. Has become significantly less popular as Facebook and Twitter have grown. *http://myspace.com*	23
news feed	The stream of status updates, links, photos, and comments from people and organizations in your network on Facebook.	21
platform	A common term for a single social network, as well as the combination of networks that form your personal or organizational social media presence.	6
post	Anything you publish through a social network, but used most commonly to refer to a blog article and, in verb form, a Facebook status update (e.g., "I posted my latest blog post on Facebook").	7
recommendation	Facebook pages allow fans to leave a recommendation about the business or organization. Likewise, LinkedIn asks users to solicit recommendations from colleagues and friends to post with their profile.	36
retweet/RT	When one Twitter user shares another user's tweet with her or his network. Introduced with "RT" and the Twitter user name of the source tweet (e.g., *RT @anglobaptist: What is the purpose of the local church?*)	39
RSS feed	Real Simple Syndication. Every blog publishes an RSS feed that allows aggregators to keep up-to-date with new content as it is produced. Visitors to a blog site can subscribe to the RSS feed so that they receive updates when new posts are added.	91

Term	Definition	Page
search engine	An online tool for searching websites for information on a particular topic or key word. [See Bing, Google.]	98
share/sharing	A feature on Facebook that allows users to repost content from a member of their network to the rest of the members of their networks.	39
shout-out	The mention of a person on Twitter, tagging her or him on Facebook, or linking to online content, generally for the purpose of praise or recognition.	39
social capital	"The collective value of all 'social networks' (who people know) and the inclinations that arise from these networks to do things for each other." [Robert Putnam, *Bowling Alone*]	81
status	A post on a personal Facebook page is called a "status update."	21
tag/tagging	A word or very short phrase that describes and indexes content in a blog post, on a website, or in other online material so it can be more easily found by search engines. On Facebook, posts and photos can be tagged with the names of friends in a person's network or group pages that a person likes. On Twitter, the hashtag symbol (#) marks searchable tags.	35
trending	When a topic on Twitter becomes very popular, it is said to be "trending" and is listed as a "trend" on the Twitter home page. Trends are often marked with a hashtagged word or phrase and can be sponsored by businesses and other organizations. They are indexed on Twitter by geographical regions.	79
tweep	Slang for a person with whom a Twitter user connects regularly on Twitter. Also, "tweople."	80

Term	Definition	Page
tweet	A post on Twitter which is limited to 140 characters, including spaces between words and punctuation.	2
tweetchat	A regularly scheduled conversation on Twitter, organized by a unique hashtag. (e.g., #chsocm marks tweets from the weekly Church and Social Media tweetchat.)	80
tweetup	A face-to-face gathering of Twitter users from a local area or with a common interest.	85
Twitter	A public social networking platform, on which people communicate in tweets 140 characters or fewer. *http://twitter.com*	1
Vimeo	A video-sharing website. Less popular than YouTube, but many prefer the video quality of Vimeo and appreciate the lack of advertizing on the site. *http://vimeo.com*	136
widget	A software application made available to users with code that can be added to other platforms, such as a website or blog. Facebook, Twitter, YouTube, and most other social networking sites provide widget code that enables a link to the site to appear on a blog or website.	83
Wikipedia	A free, online encyclopedia created and updated by volunteer users of the site. *http://en.wikipedia.org*	143
Yahoo	A web portal that offers searching capabilities, email, news, small business advertising, and social networking features. *http://yahoo.com*	104
YouTube	The web's most popular video sharing social network. Owned by Google. *http://youtube.com*	1

NOTES

Introduction

1. The terms "digital native" and "digital immigrant" were introduced by Mark Prensky in the article "Digital Natives, Digital Immigrants," *On the Horizon* (MCB Press, Vol. 9 No. 5, October 2001).

2. Elizabeth Drescher, *Tweet If You ♥ Jesus: Practicing Church in the Digital Reformation* (Harrisburg, PA: Morehouse, 2011), 17–21.

3. On this see David Kinnaman and Gabe Lyons, *Unchristian: What a New Generation Thinks About Christianity . . . and Why It Matters* (Grand Rapids, MI: Baker Books, 2007).

Chapter 1

1. Detailed images and descriptions of the Hereford *Mappa Mundi* are available at the Hereford Cathedral website: *http://www.herefordcathedral.org/visit-us/mappa-mundi-1*.

2. See Jenise Uehara Henrikson, "The Growth of Social Media: An Infographic," *Search Engine Journal*, August 30, 2011. Available online at *http://www.searchengine journal.com/the-growth-of-social-media-an-infographic/32788/*.

3. Jennifer Bergen, "Americans Spent 53.5 Billion Minutes on Facebook in May," *Geek.com*, September 13, 2011. Available online at: *http://www.geek.com/articles/geek-cetera/americans-spent-53-5-billion-minutes-on-facebook-in-may-20110913/*.

4. ComScore Data Mine, "Average Time Spent on Social Networking Sites by Geographies," June 7, 2011. Available online at: *http://www.comscoredatamine. com/2011/06/average-time-spent-on-social-networking-sites-across-geographies/*.

5. Brian Ward, "Religion Dominates Facebook Page Engagement," *All Facebook: The Unofficial Facebook Resource*, August 8, 2011. Available online at *http://www.allface-book.com/religion-dominates-facebook-page-engagement-2011-08*.

6. Mary Madden and Kathryn Kickuhr, "65% of Online Adults Use Social Networking Sites," Pew Internet & American Life Project, August 26, 2011, available online at *http://pewinternet.org/~/media//Files/Reports/2011/PIP-SNS-Update-2011.pdf*; and NetProspect, "NetProspect Social Business Report," Summer 2011, available online at *https://www.netprospex.com/np/system/files/NetProspex_SocialBusinessReport_Summer 2011.pdf*; Neilson, Inc., "State of the Social Media Report," Q3 2011, available online at *http://blog.nielsen.com/nielsenwire/social/*. Data collected September 16, 2011.

7. Sources: Ken Burbary, "Facebook Demographics Revisited—2011 Statistics." Available online at *http://www.kenburbary.com/2011/03/facebook-demographics-revisited-2011-statistics-2/; Checkfacebook.com; istrategylabs.com.*

8. Graeme McMillan, "How Many People Actually Use Twitter? Good Question," August 29, 2011. Available online at *http://techland.time.com/2011/08/29/how-many-people-actually-use-twitter-good-question/.*

9. Eryn Brown, "Using Twitter to Track People's Moods," *Los Angeles Times* (September 29, 2011). Available online at *http://articles.latimes.com/2011/sep/29/health/la-he-twitter-mood-20110930.*

10. ComScore.com, "The Netherlands Ranks #1 in Worldwide Penetration for Twitter and LinkedIn," April 2011. Available online at *http://www.comscore.com/Press_Events/Press_Releases/2011/4/The_Netherlands_Ranks_number_one_Worldwide_in_Penetration_for_Twitter_and_LinkedIn.*

11. Aaron Smith & Lee Rainie, "8% of Americans Online Use Twitter," Pew Internet & American Life Project, Dec. 9, 2010; Aaron Smith, "Twitter Update, 2011," Pew Internet & American Life Project, June 1, 2011; HeyWire Blog, *http://blog.heywire.com/2011/04/facebook-vs-twitter-demographics-infographic/.*

Chapter 2

1. Brené Brown, *The Gifts of Imperfection: Let Go of Who You Think You're Supposed to Be and Embrace Who You Are* (Center City, MN: Hazelden, 2010), 49.

2. Elizabeth Drescher, "Facebook Doesn't Kill Churches. Churches Kill Churches," *Religion Dispatches*, March 16, 2011. Available online at *http://www.religiondispatches.org/archive/atheologies/4390/facebook_doesn't_kill_churches,_churches_kill_churches/.*

3. Dan Zarrella, "Stop Talking About Yourself, Start Talking As Yourself," *Dan Zarrella*, December 13, 2010. Available online at *http://danzarrella.com/stop-talking-about-yourself-start-talking-as-yourself.html#.*

4. Adam J. Copeland, "Church Social Media Policies: An Academic Paper," *A Wee Blether,* January 3, 2011. Available online at *http://www.adamjcopeland.com/2011/01/03/church-social-media-policies-an-academic-paper/.*

5. Nielsen, "The State of the Media: Social Media Report 3Q 2011," *Nielsen.* Available online at *http://blog.nielsen.com/nielsenwire/social/.*

6. Kelly Fryer, "Pastors on Facebook: Get Real," *The Renewable Church*, February 10, 2011. Available online at *http://www.renewablechurch.com/2011/02/pastors-on-facebook-get-real.html.*

Chapter 3

1. On this, see Elizabeth Drescher, "HWJT (How Would Jesus Tweet?): Reimagining Media as Social," *Explore*, Fall 2011. Available online at *http://www.scu.edu/ignatian center/publications/explorejournal/fall2011/drescher.cfm*

2. Leonard Sweet, *The Gospel According to Starbucks: Living Life with a Grande Passion* (Colorado Springs, CO: WaterBrook Press, 2007).

3. Jennifer Preston, "Facebook Page for Jesus, With Highly Active Fans," *New York Times*, September 4, 2011.

4. Blog demographics from Sysomos, Inc., "Inside Blog Demographics," June 2010. Available online at *http://www.sysomos.com/reports/bloggers/*.

5. Douglas Quenqua, "Blogs Falling in an Empty Forest," *New York Times*, June 5, 2009, available online at *http://www.nytimes.com/2009/06/07/fashion/07blogs. html*; and Elizabeth Drescher, "New Media and the Reshaping of Religious Practice," *Immanent Frame*, March 18, 2010, available online at *http://blogs.ssrc.org/ tif/2010/03/16/new-media-and-the-reshaping-of-religious-practice/*.

6. Gary Kawasaki, *Enchantment: The Art of Changing Hearts, Minds, and Actions* (London: Penguin, 2011), Kindle Locations 2152–2154.

Chapter 4

1. See, for example, the Darkwood Brew online ministry led by Eric Elnes, which offers an online broadcast service each Sunday at *http://www.onfaithonline.tv/darkwood brew/*. Likewise, members of church communities in the virtual reality site Second Life have explored the idea of offering a virtual Eucharist. On this, see Bosco Peters, "Virtual Eucharist: Can Sacraments Work in the Virtual World?," Liturgy (Blog), June 28, 2008. Accessed online at *http://www.liturgy.co.nz/blog/virtual-eucharist/1078*. Elizabeth explored the challenges of such ministries to face-to-face worship in *Tweet If You ♥ Jesus: Practicing Church in the Digital Reformation* (Morehouse, 2011), 61–64.

2. Timothy Fry, OSB, *The Rule of St. Benedict in Latin and English with Notes* (Collegeville, MN: Liturgical Press, 1981), ch. 53:1–3.

3. Scott McLeod, "Are We Irrelevant to the Digital Global World in Which We Now Live?" *UCEA Review* 52 (Summer 2011): 1–5. Available online at *http://www.ucea. org/storage/review/Summer2011Review_lowres.pdf*.

4. Michael Wesch, "From Knowledgeable to Knowledge-able: Learning in New Media Environments," *Academic Commons*, January 7, 2009. Available online at *http://www.academiccommons.org/commons/essay/knowledgable-knowledge-able*.

5. For the full conversation and a link to the sermon, see Trip Hudgins, "The Principle Function(s) of the Local Congregation," *Conjectural Navel Gazing; Jesus in Lint Form* (blog), November 11, 2011 at *http://www.anglobaptist.org/blog/ archives/2011/11/the_principal_f_1.html*.

6. Lee Rainie, Kristen Purcell, and Aaron Smith, "The Social Side of the Internet," Pew Internet & American Life Project, January 18, 2011. Available online at *http:// www.pewinternet.org/Reports/2011/The-Social-Side-of-the-Internet.aspx*.

7. On this see Janna Quitney Anderson and Lee Raine, "The Future of Social Relations," Pew Internet & American Life Project, July 2, 2010. Available online at

http://pewinternet.org/~/media//Files/Reports/2010/PIP_Future_of_Internet_%20 2010_social_relations.pdf.

8. Robert D. Putnam, "Social Capital Primer," accessed November 11, 2011. Available online at *http://bowlingalone.com/?page_id=70.*

9. Robert Putnam, *Bowling Alone: The Collapse and Revival of American Community* (Simon and Schuster, 2001), 23.

10. Clay Shirky, *Here Comes Everybody: The Power of Organizing without Organizing* (New York: Penguin, 2008), 22.

11. Douglas Rushkoff, "Think Occupy Wall Street Is a Phase? You Don't Get It," *CNN.com*, October 5, 2011. Available at *http://www.cnn.com/2011/10/05/opinion/ rushkoff-occupy-wall-street/index.html.*

12. Shirky, *Here Comes Everybody*, 142.

13. Nadia Bolz-Weber, "Sermon on John 3:16: 'Weirdos [*Sic*] and Violence,'" *Sarcastic Lutheran Blog*, March 22, 2011. Available online at *http://sarcasticlutheran.type pad.com/sarcastic_lutheran/2011/03/sermon-on-john-316-weirdos-and-violence.html.*

Conclusion

1. Stephanie Spellers, Sermon at Grace Cathedral, San Francisco, CA, October 30, 2011. Available online at *http://www.gracecathedral.org/cathedral-life/worship/listen/ detail.php?fid=58.*

2. Pew Forum on Religion & Public Life, "U.S. Religious Landscape Survey: Religious Affiliation: Diverse and Dynamic," February 2008, 21–38. Mainline Protestant affiliation change average calculated from "Retention of Childhood Members of Protestant Religious Groups," 31.

3. Elizabeth Drescher, *Tweet If You ♥ Jesus: Practicing Church in the Digital Reformation* (Harrisburg: Morehouse, 2011), 127.

4. Anna Lenhart, et al., "Teens, Kindness and Cruelty on Social Networking Sites: How American Teens Navigate the New World of 'Digital Citizenship,'" Pew Internet & American Life Project, November 9, 2011, available online at *http://www.pewinternet.org/~/media//Files/Reports/2011/PIP_Teens_Kindness_ Cruelty_SNS_Report_Nov_2011_FINAL_110711.pdf*; and "Why Americans Use Social Media," Pew Internet & American Life Project, November 15, 2011, available online at *http://www.pewinternet.org/Reports/2011/Why-Americans-Use-Social-Media. aspx?src=prc-headline.*